Kevin Boniface

Round About Town

Uniformbooks 2018

First published 2018, reprinted 2019
Copyright © Kevin Boniface
ISBN 978-1-910010-18-1

Uniformbooks
7 Hillhead Terrace, Axminster, Devon EX13 5JL
www.uniformbooks.co.uk

Trade distribution in the UK by Central Books
www.centralbooks.com

Printed and bound by T J International, Padstow, Cornwall

Tuesday, 3 August 2010

06.30am: I can see a figure lying face-down on the pavement up ahead. I get a bit closer and I see his right arm move. He rolls briefly onto his side and back onto his front, where he lies still again. He's wearing new, clean clothes: plaid shirt, dark blue denim jeans and expensive-looking trainers. As I pass, I ask whether he's okay. He rolls onto his side again. He's young, mid-twenties, dark curly hair. "I'm just bored", he says. "Oh, as long as your okay?" I say. "Have you got a spare cig'?" "No." "Okay", and he rolls back onto his front.

I carry on up the road and into the park where a man of about sixty years old—Adidas trainers and shorts—is picking up the dog shit left by his border terrier and putting it into a little plastic bag.

Thursday, 5 August

Darrell, my neighbour, catches me as I leave for work, "Er, Kevin, I've got something to show you". He dashes inside, wiping his hands on his pinny as he goes. When he returns he stands on his step, hiding something behind his back. "Do you cook a lot of chicken?" he asks. "Not really, occasionally", I say. "Well, I've got just the thing", he says and, with a slight flourish, he produces one of those shallow tin trays that chickens come in when you buy them from a supermarket. "Marks and Spencer", he says, "It came free with the chicken". "Thanks", I say.

The pillar box outside the post office is jammed full of junk mail and takeaway flyers with obscenities scrawled all over them in blue biro. Someone has also tried to set fire to them by feeding matches through the slot. I mention it to the woman who works behind the counter, "I know! I caught her doing it", she says, "it was Mrs Armitage from Whiteley Street".

A young man in a tracksuit is cutting his own hair with a pair of blue plastic handled scissors as he walks down Cross Lane. He has no mirror and is feeling the hair at his temples with his left hand as he snips with his right.

On the landing, Irfan says the yardies had been threatening him again so during a quiet spell he nips over the road to the gun shop to buy a bulletproof vest. He returns without one, "They're four hundred quid so I didn't bother".

Tuesday, 10 August

5.30am: A man with a baby in a pram raps hard on the shutters of the news-agent's shop. A hundred yards further down the road I pass a drunk goth eating a bag of Skips.

Later, I see a woman with a cast on her leg walking up South Lane. She says she's not going to the hairdressers now because they're going to squeeze her in on Tuesday instead. She says she's off up to Julie's because she's got a seat outside.

D-MON K!D, $L!T K!D and EV!L BO¥ have all written their names on the pillar box at Reinwood.

A man with two black eyes walks up Manchester Road.

Friday, 13 August

At the newsagent's, Christine is on the till. She nods at the pile of Examiners on the counter and says "There's a new murder every day, isn't there? It's like a new craze or something". "A craze?" I say. "Yeh, you know, like a new craze from America. Like skateboarding." "Yes", I say. "Do you remember that craze for blokes hanging themselves not so long back?" says Christine. "No?" "Yes, a bit back, about six months, a year back. Between me and my ex-husband, we knew half a dozen blokes who hung themselves in the space of about three months." "Seriously?" "Two of them were on our paper-rounds" says Christine. "Blimey! I wonder what brought that on?" "I don't know. Do you remember him who built our steps? He was one, hung himself." "Really? That's terrible" I say. "I know, and the thing is everyone's always going on about them steps; the top one's too short. People are always tripping over it and then they come in here and say 'Whoever did them steps wants shooting!' What am I supposed to say to that now?"

Thursday, 26 August

I find a note in the street on my way into work. It's written in marker pen on a sheet of A4 paper. It's the third I've found bearing this message in the last six months: 'Iranian intelligence officers lick English Arse'.

Bob is back at work after a week off. I ask whether he's had a good time and he tells me his dog ate his Yorkshire pudding in a café in Grassington.

Twice today, I've been asked for directions to the Spiritualist church.

At County Foods, I hand my paperwork to the receptionist and she fills in her signature while talking on the phone, "I've got this guy on hold, he's ringing from a café in Batley. He's on about black puddings…" Suddenly, a large dog jumps up from behind the desk and starts barking at me, its front paws on the sill of the service hatch. The receptionist puts down the phone and drags the dog back down by its collar. A tall man in a suit leans in through an adjoining door and gives her a quizzical look. "Don't ask", she says. "Is it a guard dog?" says the tall man. "It's guarding me from the likes of you Alan", says the receptionist.

The chubby assistant with the heavy foundation and the glittery bits on her face at the newsagent's tells her colleague about her unfaithful boyfriend. "He said she looked better from a distance than close to but he still knobbed her, didn't he? He's got a picture of it on his phone!"

Monday, 6 September

In her garden on Hart Street, an old woman in a dressing gown empties a jug of custard onto her borders.

A young man with his hand down the front of his trousers and a bloody nose is talking to a man in a snapback cap, "Drop them two off…" he says, gesturing to two young women with low cut tops and large breasts in the back of a P-reg' VW Golf, "…then we'll go into town and get wired".

Later, in the park, I see another man with a bloody nose. He's talking to a tree.

A squirrel carries a Wagon Wheel (the chocolate kind) across Wren Street.

Thursday, 9 September

"Oh, Septimus! Oh dear! I told you to go before we came out! Oh dear", says the woman in the twin set and obvious wig to her King Charles spaniel.

Howard says he shot a rat at 6.30 this morning. He says he's pleased to have got the bugger at last but his neighbours complained about the noise.

At Slack Farm, Mr Haigh comes out of the milking shed carrying a coat at arm's length. The lining is torn out and It's completely covered in shit and straw. "Fucking cows have had us coat. They're a set of bastards" he says. "Eurgh! That's had it now, hasn't it?" I say. "Aye, normal folk would chuck it away. I'm gonna wash it." I follow him up to his front door with his mail, past the tractor with the mature ragwort growing out from under the seat and the neat row of four dead moles laid out on the garden wall. Mr Haigh tells me that moles have a very keen sense of smell and hands like people. "If you smell of fags or booze when you lay the traps you'll not catch any."

At the Community Health Centre, the receptionist bursts out through the doors into the car park and vomits next to a Honda Civic.

Back at the office, I see Irfan. He's been off work for a couple of weeks and when I ask why he tells me he's been stabbed.

Sunday, 12 September

While I'm opening the pouch box on Heatherfield Road, an old man at the bus stop comments on my bunch of keys, "You've plenty of keys there", he says.

As I'm posting the mail at the Baptist church a young man in a hooded top starts shouting something to me from the other side of the street. I can't hear him above the noise of the traffic so he shouts again. I still can't hear so he shouts a third time. And a fourth. I still can't hear, so he shouts again. I still can't hear. I go to the very edge of my pavement and he goes to his. He shouts at the top of his voice over the top of the traffic "HE ONLY GETS HOLY MAIL YOU KNOW!" "OH!" I shout back.

Inside the council flats, the window cleaner is talking to an elderly woman. She tells him she's not been well. "I've been here, there and everywhere at the hospital and they can't fathom what it is." "Oh dear, there's always summat in't there?" says the window cleaner. The woman continues, "Now they're reckoning it might be Parkinson's disease so I'm going to have to go for tests for that now too". "Oh dear, there's always summat in't there?" says the window cleaner again. "Oh, but it *is* painful in my hands." "There's always summat in't there?" "I can't even do the washing it's so painful." "There's always summat." "But I always like to say to myself 'There's always someone worse off, isn't there?'" "Oh dear, there's always summat in't there. See you next time love." The window cleaner leaves the building and shouts

up to his colleague who is cleaning windows on the first floor, "Jesus-God-Alive! I feel like slitting my wrists when I've gone in there! It's your turn next time!"

Thursday, 23 September

The man with the tartan Thermos, the pea-coat and the all-year-round woolly hat has started crossing the road when he sees me. We pass each other at 6am every morning and he's often the only other person I see as I walk into work. After a few weeks of ignoring each other, I let on and said "Morning". He didn't reply. As time went by and I persisted, he started to respond but never seemed very comfortable with it. His eyes would start flickering nervously at me from about twenty yards away, I'd say "Morning" and he'd emit an awkward choking sound accompanied by a twitchy sideways glance. Now he crosses the road and keeps his eyes fixed on the pavement.

A man in a hooded North Face jacket, elaborately top-stitched jeans and Nike trainers is smoking a cigarette and fiddling with a Blackberry on the steps at the entrance to the flats. I say hello as I approach, assuming he'll move across so I can get past. He doesn't. He doesn't respond or even glance up. I squeeze through, my bag scraping against his knee, but he still doesn't move or acknowledge my presence in any way. When I come out of the flats ten minutes later, the man is still there, smoking another cigarette and thumbing his Blackberry. I say hello again, he looks up, squints, pulls on his cigarette and looks down again.

Two overweight men in their thirties are talking as they walk past me on Ings Way, "I bet I fucking could", says one. "I bet you fucking couldn't", says the other. "I bet I fucking could." "You fucking couldn't." "I fucking could." "You fucking couldn't." "I bet I fucking could…"

A woman in flat shoes and a very full skirt stops me in the street to tell me she's been to the ninetieth birthday party of her pianist, "I'm in the choir at the Methodist. The cake was in the shape of a grand piano. It was sponge but it was lovely and moist".

Sunday, 3 October

A young man wearing a yellow vest, faded red boxer shorts and fluffy yellow slippers is sitting on my neighbour's front step in the rain at 5.30am.

I see a fox on Station Road.

On the bus, I overhear a man telling his companion that he shat himself in bed after drinking too many Turbo Diesels in the pub.

Mrs Shaw gives me a bag of homegrown tomatoes. She says she's completely self-sufficient as far as tomatoes are concerned.

Dr Groves opens his front door to take his mail. "It's a reasonable day by the looks of it", he says.

Mr Briggs pulls up to tell me he's off to Oldham today. He pauses, then says "Actually, I tell a lie, I'm off to the office, then to Meltham and then to Oldham. I'm working on the precinct there, it's a right bastard to park". That's all he says, then he gets back into his Suzuki Carry and drives away.

At the Chartered Accountants', a chubby white male chartered accountant with brown plastic-rimmed glasses, a white shirt and a grey suit is talking to a slim white female chartered accountant in a white shirt and a slightly lighter grey suit. "Did you get through Chapeltown all right yesterday?" asks the man. "I know! I didn't see a single white face!" says the woman biting her lip. "I bet you didn't want to stop at the lights did you?" "No", says the woman, "I pushed my door locks down!" She mimes twisting around and pushing down the door lock. "Absolutely terrifying", she says.

Mrs Gaunt waves to me from her first-floor window with a tenon saw in her hand.

Places I've seen the Cross of St George today: 1. Painted across the bonnet of a white baker's van. 2. On a flag flying from a dead tree in a garden on Manse Drive. 3. On a flag flying from the Foresters Arms pub. 4. Painted on a drain cover by the back door of a house in Cowlersley. 5. On a flag flying from what used to be The Green Cross real ale pub but is now a Sex Encounter Club with blacked out windows and plans for a sauna.

Saturday, 9 October

5.30am: A man is walking towards me in the park. He's singing loudly to himself and occasionally performing a kind of shimmy. He stops to take a long drag on his cigarette, briefly looks up and notices me coming down the path. At this point, he begins to cough in what seems like a fake way and when he starts walking again, he does so with a pronounced swagger and an expressionless face.

Trizzle and N. Smith have both written their names on the May Street pouch box.

On the estate, I knock at a house to deliver a registered parcel. A man answers. He's carrying a little boy in a duffle coat, mittens and a woollen hat, "Oh thanks, mate, that's great, I've been waiting for that. Excellent!" He puts down the little boy to sign for the package and a slim women in a vest top peers around the door. Her eyes widen, "Is that your new phone? Fucking hell you jammy cunt! Mine took fucking ages. Fucking hell!"

According to the large A1 laminated poster entitled 'The Toby Grill Hall Of Fame', Mick has served 994 drinks and Kerry over 400 meals so far this week.

A man who looks a bit like Tony Hancock stops me in Kirkwood Drive to ask whether I know why there is so much bird muck on the roofs of the bungalows there.

Tuesday, 12 October

A man is lying on his side on his asphalt driveway manicuring the edge of his lawn with a pair of shears. Half his backside is showing. He rolls over onto his back to say hello.

Leylandii, berberis, box hedge and open-plan lawns. Stone built bungalows with feature arches and patio-doors, swirly carpets and telephone tables. Staffordshire ladies on the window sills.

"Did you hear about the burglary two doors down? They're on holiday. They didn't draw their curtains, didn't set their alarm. What did they expect?"

Rockery islands and miniature conifers. Limestone and alpines.

Locks on doors, locks on windows, locks on cars, locks on bikes, locks on sheds, locks on greenhouses, locks on gates… Two cars on the drive and nobody home.

Women walk the streets in fleeces and overactive Reactolites. Pulling on North Faces as it starts to drizzle. Swinging little bags of dog shit as they stride on towards Strawberry Drive in spotted Barbour wellingtons. Dragging a growling, clipped schnauzer as it tries to hold its ground.

"Why are you like this with the postman? He's usually so placid and lovely, aren't you?" she says, without looking up.

In the week, it's older, retired men with tucked-in shirts and side partings. They lie down underneath Range Rovers or fine-tune their lawns. They say "What's she been ordering now?" about "the missus" who sometimes comes outside in her specs and unusually coloured hair. "Have you seen the postman?" she says as she sets down a tall glass and a

Hobnob. At the weekends it's younger men who stand on their lawns in casual sportswear holding power tools. They say "All right mate?" while 'the missus', in her navy-blue polo shirt with the buttons undone, holds a spaniel by the collar. There are one or two children but they are at nursery except on Saturday when one of them gets strapped into the seat of his grandad's Ford Focus and taken to the United game. His grandma waves him off, she already has her pinny on.

Thursday, 21 October

On my way into work, I see a bat, an owl, the short woman with the sweat-shirt and the peroxide perm who goes through the bins in the park and, on the pavement outside the Mortgage Introducer and International Flights shop on John William Street, a women's block heeled boot.

At the house with the broken porch, a boy of about three or four is sitting on the window sill wearing nothing but a nappy and drinking milk from a baby bottle. I knock at the door and a thin woman in her forties with braces on her teeth flings it open and shouts "Toilet!" before adding, "Oh sorry love, I thought you were someone else".

Mr Briggs intercepts me in his Suzuki Carry. He asks whether I've ever toured Scotland by coach. I say I haven't. He tells me his wife saw an advert in *The Examiner*: "Up one side and down the other. Five hotels in a week!" Mr Briggs goes on at some length about his reservations about coach travel. "A sore arse… compulsory seat belts… steamed-up windows that you can't see out of… the lack of decent toilet facilities… If you get sat next to a knobhead…" and so forth. "I said all this to her", he explains, "but she'd already gone and booked it, hadn't she? Her and Barbara had cooked it up together, hadn't they? So the four of us went

together: me, the missus and Gary and Barbara. And do you know what?" says Mr Briggs looking up at me from over his wire rims. "What?" I say. "We had a real time! It were fantastic! We've been another, one, two, three, four times since!" He tells me about some of the exploits they've had: "They're only allowed to drive for a couple of hours at a time these days so we always have t'chance to have a coffee or a tea". And how he'd got around the "seat belt problem". "If you plug the belt into the thing before you get into your seat and then just sit on it, the driver's alarm doesn't go off. He'd had to tell me a couple of times over the tannoy before I figured that out." Mr Briggs chuckles and does an impression of the bus driver, "Passenger number forty-four, could you fasten your belt please!" I tell Mr Briggs that I once travelled from London to Paris by coach and I found it quite tough going. I start to elaborate with an amusing anecdote from the journey but he cuts me short saying, "Anyway, I'm off to Leeds now" and he drives away.

Monday, 25 October

As I drive up Crosland Road I see a colleague being attacked by a fat black Labrador with a fluorescent green collar. He manages to protect himself with his mail pouch before kicking the dog in the head. The dog runs off and my colleague gives me the thumbs up as I pass.

At the army surplus shop, a customer asks the proprietor whether he has a hat like Michelle wore in *'Allo 'Allo*. The proprietor says he hasn't.

As I make my way up the front path of a house in Greenwood Street, the door opens and a large aggressive looking German shepherd runs out of it towards me. Fortunately, the dog is attached by a length of blue rope to its owner, a man in his fifties in a torn anorak. The man is dragged down his steps and several feet up the path towards me before he

regains his footing and restrains the dog. "Don't worry", he says, "He doesn't bite as a rule, It's your bag. He doesn't like postmen or people with bags". The dog barks and snarls and pulls the man another foot or so up the path. "When I take him down on the field I have to have a good look around to make sure there's no one about with a bag otherwise he'll think it's the postman and he'll have them." "Oh", I say. "Yeah, it's just bags—and postmen. Funny, isn't it?"

As I round the corner into Lawton Street, a young boy of about eight or nine speeds off down the hill on a BMX. Two other boys jump up and down excitedly. One of them points after the BMX boy and shouts to me, "He's shit his pants! His bum is wet!"

11.30am: A large woman in pyjamas comes out of the shop holding a packet of Lambert and Butler cigarettes and a copy of *The Sun*. She's having a conversation via speaker-phone. She holds her phone in front of her face while she shouts into it in a southern accent: "... and then she says 'Fuck you! It's over! Now fuck off!' You gotta love her, haven't you? Anyway, don't forget your key... Love you loads and loads... Byee!"

Half-an-hour later, I see the woman again. She's smoking one of her Lambert and Butlers in the garden at number 17 with two other women in pyjamas.

I watch an aggressive stand-off develop between two young men. It begins with the usual cursing and swearing but escalates into something quite unusual, ending thus: "You're a fucking moo cow!" "You fucking moo cow!" "MOOOO COOOW!" "You're a moo cow!" "MOOOOOOO COOOOOOOW!" "You're a moo cow!" With that, one of the men chases the other up the road and into a house, slamming the door behind him.

I knock at the door of a house on the estate. I hear the back door open and a Border terrier runs around the corner, squats at my feet and starts pissing. I step away as the dog's owner comes out saying, "Don't worry love, she'll not bother you".

Tuesday, 2 November

An old man is cleaning egg from his front door. He tells me that some vandals threw it at the house on Halloween. He says he'd like to pin them down by the throat with the handle of his broom and stamp on it.

At a house on Sycamore Close, the bald man wearing motorcycle leathers and a Bluetooth earpiece says "Hold on John", and makes a "Do I need to sign for it?" sign by pretending to write in the air in front of his face with an imaginary pen. I make a sign for "No" by shaking my head and I hand over his package. The man gives me an emphatic thumbs up and continues with his Bluetooth conversation with John, "...the thing is mate..."

The old lady whose light blue fine knit cardigan exactly matches the colour of both her garage door and her meter housing box is very pleased with her parcel of garden bulbs, she says it's "just the right size".

Twice in succession during my parcel delivery, the door is answered by a middle-aged woman with a broken arm.

The German shepherd at the bottom of the street seems particularly keen to get at me today. It's on its hind legs at the gate barking and snarling. The fur on its back is on end and it doesn't take its eyes off me as I deliver the mail to the neighbouring houses. As I approach, it becomes apoplectic, barking furiously. A thin woman with a blonde perm and skinny jeans opens the door of the house, runs up to the dog and grabs it by the collar. She pulls it down from the gate but it struggles loose and leaps back up to continue its frenzied display. The woman makes a second attempt to grab the dog and this time she manages to keep ahold long enough for me to pass over her mail. "Thank you!" she shouts in a strong eastern European accent, "She is very friendly dog!"

As I queue in the Co-op to buy a new jar of peanut butter and some Mini Cheddars, the woman on the till shouts to a colleague, "Lisa, would you class this as quiet?" Lisa breaks off from her customer and briefly glances around the shop, "Umm, yeah, I reckon". My till woman shouts back to Lisa, "Good, I need a wee".

I see another headless pigeon. This one is on Yew Tree Road near the junction with Weatherill Road.

Saturday, 6 November

"Have you got owt for me?" says the bald man with the big jeans and the paintbrush in his hand. I hand him an envelope from the DVLA. "Car tax", says the man. "Have a guess how much—go on. I bet it'll be £225." "What kind of car have you got?" I ask. "A V70. I can't be doing with small cars. What have you got?" "A little Skoda. It's old", I say. "Crappy little things. No disrespect to you, I just can't be doing with them." "I've never bought a new car", I say. "I've bought twenty-four. I've got two at the moment. The Volvo and a BMW. I need two because I'm going up to Scotland for a few days." The man tears open the envelope and unfolds the letter. "£205. Not as bad as I thought! It's a lot though, isn't it? It adds up; it's four quid a week that. I was self-employed for twenty-five year but I've passed all the work on to someone else, just walked away from it. Still got my name running around on fifteen vans mind." The man waves his paintbrush at his driveway, "just got a quote to get that re-surfaced: five and a half grand. Would you pay that?" "No", I say. "No, but even if you had the money, would you?" "I suppose I might. I don't know." "I'm seventy year old. What's the point? I'd only be doing it for someone else, wouldn't I?" The man looks up at the window frame he's painting and says "Anyway, you'd better let me get on. See you lad".

The young couple with the tattoos and the toddler at number 201 have fastened a VW badge to their front door.

A skinhead in combat fatigues who is smoking weed asks me for directions to his own house.

Friday, 12 November

On my way into work at 5.15am I see two skinny men rolling a lorry wheel up Church Street. They are soaking wet and panting loudly.

At the Toby Grill, a man in a blue fleece jacket and jeans rummages through the box of Remembrance Day poppies on the bar while the barmaid pulls him a pint of bitter. "Where are the pins? You need a pin in it", he says. "They never came with any. I'm surprised we've got rid of so many" says the barmaid.

At the Grange, I lift the flap of the letterbox and half a dozen large black flies drop out into a stream of run-off that carries them struggling away down the driveway.

The man fitting metal window screens to a vacant house on Elmfield Avenue asks me whether I'd like to buy some trainers. I say no.

I pass a large pair of Eurimco pumps discarded on a country lane.

The woman at number 36 tells me about her wealthy neighbour's recent home improvements: "It's unbelievable! He got an interearier [sic] designer in who is a gay from Leeds so it looks amazing!"

Two young men in their twenties talk on the bus: "Were you on Black Ops last night?" "No, I was going to but I had to go up to the shop to get a tin opener."

Tuesday, 16 November

The man walking in front of me with the shaved head, tracksuit pants and the shiny blouson jacket stops to pick up a packet of sodden cigarettes from the gutter. He opens it but he can't get at the contents because they're all stuck together. He tears at the packet, peels away a wet cigarette from the cluster, puts it in his mouth and makes repeated attempts to light it.

A man with a splint on his wrist, wearing glasses and smoking a pipe says "It's a nice spot round here". Just around the corner, I see a massive red toadstool and I run over a squirrel. Ten minutes later another man who is wearing glasses and smoking a pipe (but without a splint on his wrist) says "How do?" and asks me for directions to Bradley Farm.

A bit later I trip over the wellington boot belonging to the man who is practising the drums with the window open and Mrs Sykes says she's glad it's a nice day and that junk mail is a bit of a pain but she supposes it keeps me in work.

I see my first domestic Christmas tree of the year. It has plain white lights.

Tuesday, 23 November

Someone has stolen the roof from Bradley Farm.

The sign above the door at MPC North Ltd says 'mpc north: managing people's choices'. The reception area is staffed by people in military fatigues with laptops on their knees.

At the park homes on the moor, a woman in an old fleece jacket with a picture of a wolf on it tells me I'm a good postman because she's seen me pick up an elastic band I dropped. She tells me that my colleagues just leave them on her path. The wolf woman's friend—salmon pink anorak, big set platinum hair and a plastic rain hood—says

"Ignore her love, she's like this," and the wolf woman says, "No I'm not".

At Mr Haigh's, I have to step over a dead calf to get to his front door today.

An old Ford Ka pulls up next to me. In the front is a smartly dressed couple, he in a camel hair coat with suede collars and her with a tidy perm and a large beaded necklace. In the back is another man in a beige anorak. They are all in their seventies, maybe eighties. The driver winds down his window and shouts over in a southern accent, "It's good to see a good healthy postman!" I kind of nod. The man goes on "I've got a man here…" He gestures over his shoulder at the man in the anorak. "… and I'm bringing him to see his child-hood, er, all the good people!" I look at the anorak man in the back, he's pulling faces at the driver like a petulant teen-ager and mock punching the back of his seat. "Bye bye!" says the driver, and he waves and drives away.

"A load of poofs live there", the driver of the bin wagon says to me, pointing to number 20. All the bin men laugh and say "See you, mate" as they drive off.

Wednesday, 1 December

A woman with unseasonably sheer tights feeds pigeons from a Jack Fulton Frozen Value carrier bag at 6am.

The woman at the bus stop says it's "niptorious" today.

The three young people in front of me in a heavy snow shower are in conversation: "She's dead young. They'd better make sure she doesn't get fucking pregnant" says the thin white girl with the scraped back ponytail and skinny jeans. "I know!" says the Asian boy with the saggy jeans and quilted jacket. "I need a fucking car!" says the thin white girl. "I can get you one for £135. It's alright, it's got a nice CD player or I can sort you out a USB if you want." says the Asian boy. "I don't

care as long as it goes, I've got to be in fucking town for half-one." "It should be £200 but I'll sort it for you for £135 if you definitely want it. Do you definitely want it?" "Of course I fucking do! I've got to be in fucking town, haven't I?" "Okay", says the Asian boy, "I'll bring it you round later". The third member of the group, the thin black girl with the cerise pink dressing gown and the Ugg boots doesn't say anything, she just walks alongside with her arms folded.

I suggest to a woman who is clearing her path in the blizzard that it must be a bit like painting the Forth bridge. She says she doesn't know.

A skinny Irishman in his fifties with a roll-up, a greasy ducktail and a diso-bedient sheltie sings as he passes me, "Postman, postman don't be slow, be like Elvis, go man go!" then he stops, turns around, and asks, "Did you like that?"

A young man in a hooded top and an Alfa Romeo 147 struggles to get traction in the snow. Fortunately, two more young men in hooded tops come running over, "We'll give you a push, you cunt!" and they do, right to the top of the hill. Next, a middle-aged woman in a fleece jacket and a Lodge's Pharmacy van with 'Celebrity Slim Weight Loss Program' written on it comes around the corner at the bottom and also struggles to get up the hill. This time the two young men in hooded tops shout to the thin white girl with the skinny jeans and the thin black girl with the cerise pink dressing gown who have appeared at the bottom of the street, "You two can push her!" and they walk away.

Tuesday, 7 December

The man who regularly shouts at the top of his voice from the flats at 5.30am was screaming instead this morning.

An unusual silver/grey fibreglass box has been left on Park Drive South. It's about a foot square and on the lid it says "This is it Martin" in black marker pen.

At the newsagent's, a customer tells the Asian proprietress about some neighbours who'd made him a curry, "They had a two week holiday in Pakistan, or India, I can't remember which, one or the other. Anyway, when they got back they invited me and the missus round for a curry and oh! It were bang-on! It really was superb!"

Outside, two school mums talk as they pick their way around the torn mattress, the divan bed base and the purple vest top in the icy puddle, "You're walking like a mong" says one. "I know!" says the other "I need a wee desperately".

A man with a leather jacket, blue tracksuit bottoms, black trainers, a bulbous nose, a grey moustache and a black baseball cap comes out of The Caledonian Café and belches loudly. The smell of liver and onions drifts along the bus queue.

A see a rat run across Heaton Road.

I saw my abusive neighbour again today, he was telling a learner driver to fuck off.

I need some waterproof socks.

Sunday, 12 December

5.30am: A young woman in a frock coat shouts to me from across the street, "Postman Pat! My daughter hates you!"

"It's like a bottle for you isn't it lad? Mind how you go." says the old man in the cardigan and the scarf when I almost lose my footing on an icy pavement.

I see Rod Singleton in a bobble hat, chipping ice from his driveway with a spade. He says the weathermen are talking out of their fucking arses when they tell us it's going to get warmer next week.

"Normally he cleans that path; he's a taxi driver. It's shocking is that for his wife", says the man who looks a bit like

he's from the 1970s when I slip over on his neighbour's path.

"I've lived here for forty year and I've never seen a single person come down here with a bit of salt. It's disgusting!" says the elderly man with the combover and the zip-up rib-knit raglan cardigan with suede elbow patches.

A woman in a big black coat rounds the corner and crashes her buggy into my ankles. She doesn't say anything or even look up, she just reverses a bit and goes around me.

A tall, slim woman in her mid-forties with a dyed black bob, knee-length boots, and skinny jeans walks up Moor End Road past a large snow sculpture of a cock and some balls. Arms outstretched, face raised up towards the sky and eyes shut tight, she sings along loudly to Lady Gaga on her mp3 player.

Monday, 20 December

I'm still having to step over last year's dead Christmas tree to get to the letterbox at number 87 on the estate.

A woman with tight jeans and a furry hat with ear flaps mistakes me for a colleague who recently featured in *The Daily Examiner* for doing the shopping for some of his elderly customers during the cold spell. She tells me how much old Mr Mallinson appreciated me getting his fags for him.

I hand over a parcel to a man in his fifties with some keys on his belt. It's obviously a Christmas present: "Bloody Hell! Someone's got money to burn" he says. "I'm a miserable sod, aren't I?" he adds before laughing and saying "Thank you, my man" three times in a West Midlands accent and then shutting the door.

Just past the interior designer's house with the UPVC porch and the fake leaded lights in a stylised tulip pattern, about ten yards down from where he parks his white Astra with the body kit and the white circular cardboard air freshener which dangles from the rearview mirror and has the word 'AIR' cut out of it in Helvetica Bold, opposite the red brick inter-war semi called 'UP 'EM HALL' with the three-wheeled motorcycle on the drive, half buried in the pile of mucky snow across from the house with the six-foot-high inflatable Homer Simpson wearing a Santa hat, I discover I can find eternal peace of mind from just £28.00 per annum (according to the promotional leaflet about insuring memorial stones and headstones I find there).

Sunday, 2 January 2011

5.30am: I follow a tall thin man in a hooded top down John William Street, his hands deep in his pockets. He's drunk, and on several occasions staggers the full width of the generous pavements and trips off the kerb into the road.

On the bus, the man with the tidy goatee says he had to go straight to bed after watching *The Bourne Supremacy*: "I was fucked! What a film! It was even better than James Bond".

I ask Julian whether he's had a good Christmas. He says it was a quiet one up until one of his neighbours was shot dead by the police after a noisy twenty-four-hour siege.

At the house with the incomplete decking and the broken television in the garden, there's a sticker on the letterbox that reads "If it's too loud you're too old".

Other stickers today: "Hello, Welcome. Now piss off!" and "My Rottweiler kills chavs".

A grey Renault Clio passes at high speed on the wrong side of the road. Five police cars follow. An old man says "Bloody Hell, Look at that!" and an old woman waves her fist in the air and shouts something incomprehensible.

I enter the firm of engineers through the door marked 'Security and Fitness Centre'.

"The bloody fox has got at us turkey carcass", says Mr Smith who is clearing up the mess in his driveway.

Around the perimeter of Mr Mahmood's otherwise completely barren concreted-over gardens are arranged twelve four-pint plastic milk containers. They are positioned equidistant from one another and are three-quarters filled with water.

Tuesday, 11 January

A man falls asleep in the driver's seat of a silver MG while reading a copy of the Daily Star: "PREGNANT POSH PRAYS FOR A PRINCESS".

"I don't talk to him. Kick it down the street", says the tall man in his fifties with grey hair and a paint-splattered sweatshirt when I ask him if he'll take a parcel in for his neighbour.

A red Ford Ka drives past at high speed.

On Mr Haigh's garden wall today: A Ewbank carpet sweeper with a broken handle, a handful of straw, a television set, a tin of dog food (half-empty and wrapped in polythene), two Jerry cans and a three-foot square wooden crate filled with cooking pots and utensils. Mr Haigh comes out to meet me and I mention the strong winds we've been having. "It's always windy up here lad", says Mr Haigh, "Up here's the windiest place in the country. That's how come they put all them turbines up. It's the windiest in Britain and Britain's the windiest in Europe so it must be the windiest place in Europe round here".

I find a copy of *A Brief Illustrated Guide to Understanding Islam* in a puddle on Fitzwilliam Street.

I see the red Ford Ka again, still speeding but going the other way this time.

A man in plastic-rimmed glasses, a hi-vis anorak and a flat cap that's pulled down so hard it looks like a tweed beanie, asks me whether I know one of his friends. "What does he look like?" I ask "What did he look like" the man corrects me, "he died eight years ago".

I see the red Ford Ka again. It has been abandoned half on the pavement with its near-side front wing smashed into a wall.

Tuesday, 18 January

I follow a coach up Bradford Road. The livery on the back reads, 'Stotts... taking people to places'.

At work, there's been a bag of Silver Spoon Granulated Sugar cable-tied to a ceiling joist for five years. No one remembers how it got there.

"The most embarrassing thing is when you're in a public space and you can't stop laughing", says the young woman in the long taupe tasselled skirt. She is talking with a small group of Jehovah's Witnesses who have convened in the street outside the Druid and the Witch of the End of Time's house.

On the radio, Barbara Dickson explains that when she was young, she decided she was "gonna show 'em" because she failed her 11+ exam. I change to a channel where the presenter is introducing a quiz. The contestant is a stuntwoman who says she once gave up the job for a year but missed the adrenalin rush too much. The presenter says this is fascinating. I turn over the radio again. This time the presenter says "Now it's time for Rock, Shop and Recover on The Pulse of West Yorkshire: your chance to win tickets to see Kylie live in concert!"

At the sheet metal engineers, I hand a parcel to a large man with a greasy face and blue overalls. I ask his name but don't catch his reply. "Sorry, what was

that?" I ask. "Pardon" he says. "What?" I say. "Pardon. P.A.R.D.O.N" he says, "Mr Pardon".

The weather brightens as I arrive at the golf club. A pheasant calls from the undergrowth and the greenkeeper has parked up his wheelbarrow to scratch his back on a fence post. Outside the clubhouse, a man in a suit strides across the car park carrying a large crystal chandelier, and a grey-haired man wearing a v-neck sweater waves to me as he drives past in a cream and black Morgan.

Sunday, 23 January

"His fan belt's slipping isn't it, eh?" says the man to his baby as a car squeals past. He looks down at the baby again, widens his eyes and says, "Yeees! Is his fan belt slipping? It is, isn't it? His fan belt's slipping. Yeees".

The note masking taped to the door explains that the chip shop is closed due to ill health although Peter's Computers which operates out of the same building is accessible via the telephone number provided. In the rowan tree on the pavement outside, there is a flock of about thirty waxwings.

I tear my trousers on a rusty fridge as I edge up a garden path between an overflowing wheelie bin and a pile of dog shit.

An old man shouts me from across the street, "Postman!" he says sternly. I make my way over. "When are you going to deliver my bus pass! It's been a week now!" says the man angrily. "A week since what?" I ask. "Since I went down to the bus station and filled in the card. They had a fiver off me and I've heard nowt from them since!" "Have they definitely posted it?" I ask. "How should I know?" says the man.

I see the waxwings again. This time they are in the tree by the flats where the skinny Asian man with the grey jeans and studded belt is trying to gain access by shouting Raymond.

Tuesday, 1 February

Mr Briggs pulls up to ask where the usual postman is. I tell him he's off work with an upset stomach. "One of our lads had the shits last week", says Mr Briggs, and then, without waiting for a response, he says "Right, I'm going", and he speeds off, spinning the wheels of his Suzuki Carry on the greasy old millstone setts.

The only other person under the age of retirement around here today is the builder who is converting the barn on the edge of the moor. His yellow and black heavy duty site radio plays 'Baggy Trousers' by Madness while he stands with his hand down the front of his trousers talking to the woman with the brown Labrador, the NY ski hat and the cerise pink walking socks. He tells her how much he enjoys reading books about the second world war: "...could be anything from somebody's memoirs to an account of a battle. As long as it's not fiction, I'm not arsed about that", he explains.

Thursday, 10 February

I give a colleague a lift home and he tells me about his brother, a shopfitter who flies model aircraft in his spare time. Apparently, the other night he was picked up by the police while waiting for a bus in the early hours and had no idea why. After four hours in a cell he overheard the duty sergeant telling the arresting officers they'd never make a case for loitering at a bus stop and they let him go.

"Yes, we found the best opticians", says the primary school girl with the long blond hair and the elasticated waistband as she shows her friend her new glasses. "Which one?" her friend asks. "Erm, I, I can't remember what it's called. It had a grey sign." "Specsavers?" "No, they've got a green sign. I can't remember. Anyway, I'm saying they were good but I'm still waiting for my Playboy case, aren't I?"

At one of the big houses by the golf course, the man who answers the door smells of Brasso.

A woodpecker is trying to make a hole in a telegraph pole on Lea Lane.

Mr Whitwam has cordoned off the driveway of his static caravan with a length of white plastic chain stretched between two traffic cones that he has sprayed silver. He kneels on a large foam cushion insert from an old settee while he scrapes moss from between his pink herringbone setts. His Jaguar is parked on the road.

A couple are having sex in the back of a plumber's van by the park.

Tuesday, 15 February

At the bus stop. Woman in her forties: "I'm not gonna be in tomorrow, I'm going to a concert." Man in his fifties: "What concert are you going to?" Woman: "Shaky." Man: "Shaky? What's Shaky?" Woman: (exasperated). "Shakin' Stevens! I was that exhausted after Bad Manners, I booked the day off this time." Man: "Shakin' Stevens? I had one of his LPs I think. I think it was rubbish. Did he sing 'Green Door'?" Woman: "Yes." Man: "It was rubbish that." Woman: "Well I won't be in anyway."

Mr Haigh has stuck some large COME ON ENGLAND stickers on his wheelie bins (his normal one and his recycling one).

The builder working on a new porch is singing the Simply Red song, 'For Your Babies' very loudly. He breaks off briefly to say "Alright, pal" without looking up as I walked down the garden path.

A woman stops me in the street to tell me she can smell toast.

I get stuck in the lift at the flats for half an hour until the engineer comes to open the door.

There's been a tangerine in the gutter on Bradford Road all week and yesterday I saw two bananas, one in Cote Lane and one in New Hey Road near the roundabout at Mount. This morning I saw a full bunch of bananas in Cote Lane and twenty or so eggs smashed in the gutter of Heaton Road.

The man who sleeps in his car on Mucky Lane has got a new one, a silver Rover 75.

Wednesday, 23 February

Mrs Hussain is on a treadmill watching telly again. She answers the door with a water bottle in her hand.

An old man shouts me from the first floor of the flats. He asks how long it'll be before he gets his post. "About half an hour", I say. "Hurry up lad, I need to go out! I'm already late, I've been waiting for you!" He's dressed in pyjamas.

A man in his sixties wearing jeans, slippers, a faded purple vest and an impressive tan says "Hello buddy" as he cuts his fingernails in the street. "She sends us outside to clip these", he explains.

An elderly white man with elbow patches on his cardigan and no teeth shouts me from the house across the street. I cross over to him and he hands me some mail saying "It's my address right enough but there's never been anyone of that name living here. I've lived here since this was built". I look at the top envelope. He's underlined the Asian name on it in green ink. "Go see him eight doors down with the BMW and the Juliet window; he's a foreigner, he might know". I take the mail and apologise for the mis-delivery but point out that I am obliged to deliver the mail as addressed, "For all I know, someone else could have moved in..." I explain. The old man cuts me off, rolls his eyes and says "You might think I'm a bit simple but if something says I.C.I on it, you don't deliver it to David Brown's do you?" He mimes studying an address. He looks down at an imaginary letter

in one hand, strokes his chin with the other, a cartoon wide-eyed simpleton look on his face. "I would if it was addressed to I.C.I at David Brown's address, yes", I say. "Well", says the man irritably "All you need to know is that while this sign is on this door it's me who lives here and no-one else!" And he stabs his finger at the engraved brass plaque screwed to the door frame that reads "IF YOU'VE NOT BEEN INVITED, YOU'D BETTER HAVE A DAMN GOOD REASON FOR KNOCKING AT THIS DOOR".

I wait to cross the road. The man who wears black polo-neck jumpers and never opens his curtains is also waiting to cross on the other side. Another man whose name is Johno (according to the sign in the windscreen of his wagon) stops and waves us both across. As we pass one another, the polo-neck man looks up at me and says "Hello, my friend".

Saturday, 5 March

I arrive at work early so I make a cigarette and stand on the pavement to smoke it. After a minute or so, a blue tit flies out from a tree and lands on the wing mirror of the Citroën Picasso parked in front of me. It hops down onto the bottom lip of the mirror-casing and perches there facing the glass, appearing to admire its reflection. After a few seconds, it flies to the mirror of the next parked car and does the same thing, and then again onto the third before it disappears back among the shrubs in the church gardens. I ask the man on the corner who is checking the soles of his shoes for dog shit whether he saw it, but he didn't.

Yesterday, I said hello to a man in his garden and he seemed to blank me. Today, he was there again, so I said hello again. This time he glanced up briefly to say "Now then" and continued raking his leaves.

I ask the woman in her early thirties whether she'll take a parcel for her next door neighbour. She refuses: "I don't really know them and they're just renting so, you know?"

I comment on the fluffiness of a dog to its owner as she passes me in the street. The woman stops but the dog starts towards me, growling. The woman yanks on the dog's lead and says "They're not right friendly aren't Chows. If he's ever out in the garden, you'd best not go in".

There's been a bouquet of flowers (still in cellophane) on the doorstep of number 67 all week. The man who lives there must know about them because he's been out working in his garden every day.

As I walk up the path, I shout hello to the window cleaner at number 94 but he doesn't respond. When I come back down, he's walking across the lawn to get his buckets. He doesn't look up

from under the peak of his woolly cap as he passes me but he slaps the back of one hand against the palm of the other several times and says, "Seems to be getting fucking colder". I think he's talking to me because there's nobody else around.

I see an old colleague in the street. He tells me a mutual friend who I haven't seen for years has died in a road accident: "I was at me dad's, polishing me boots when I heard", he says.

Two young men in hooded tops are fastening some blue flashing lights to the roof of a car. They each have an upturned bucket to stand on so they can reach.

The receptionist is on the phone: "I've got James from SL Recruitment on the line… Do you want anything to do with him? If I tell him you're in a meeting he'll just keep ringing me and… Okay…" Click. "Hello, James. He says he doesn't need anything at the moment so

I should give it a good long while before you ring again… That's all right. Bye bye." Click.

Back in town, a man with his cap on backwards and a cast on his leg is repeatedly gobbing on the path in the church gardens while his girlfriend (baby blue tracksuit and ponytail) is doubled over laughing at him. The man swings for her with one of his crutches but hits a pigeon instead which causes his girlfriend to collapse onto the floor in hysterics.

Sunday, 13 March

In the office, Adam is telling Nathan about the curries he's eaten over the weekend: "Balti Friday night, Pathia Saturday night and on Sunday I went round to a mate's house and we had a nice Rogan Josh. Not a bad weekend". "Blimey, I bet you're back on the fruit now! Mind you, I suppose they're not too bad for you, curries, are they?"

Says Nathan. "Depends what you fire in with 'em, doesn't it, kid?" says Adam without looking up from his work; he's standing on a box slotting letters into the top row of his frame (he's not particularly short but he says it makes his arm ache otherwise).

A red kite (the bird kind) drifts along the tree line above the road as the woman with the picture of an alien on her sweatshirt approaches me with her two boxer dogs. As she gets closer, the dogs snarl and bark at me. Without looking up, the woman shouts "Shut up! It's a man, not a Martian!"

I slip on a flight of greasy green York-stone steps. I end up at the bottom, lying on my back with my feet on the patio, slightly winded. I tell the owner about it. "Are they slippy?" he asks and hands me a mis-delivered letter from the day before.

At one of the sheltered bungalows on the estate, the old woman with the grey perm, faded blue anorak and American tan tights is putting out her wheelie bin. It's decorated with a large stripy orange and green sticker that says 'Pimp My Bin!' in a graffiti style font.

On my way down to the farm, I see a freshly killed blue tit in the middle of the lane. On my way back up five minutes later, it has gone.

Someone has written 'Retard' in the dirt on the side of old Mr Richardson's new Honda CR-V.

A rabbit runs across my path in the same place as it did yesterday.

On the estate, a boy of about five is playing on a scooter in the street. "Are you going to my house?" He asks. "Yes", I say and he throws down his scooter and runs inside shouting "Wait there!" Moments later, I see him through the window of the front room wrestling an agitated Jack Russell terrier from the back of the settee. A door slams and the boy comes running back outside. "It's our dog", he says, "I had to lock him in, he hates postmans".

Friday, 18 March

Yesterday, There was a house brick wrapped in silver foil and two metal dessert spoons on the bench on Fitzwilliam Street. This morning, the spoons have gone but the house brick is still there.

Julie from the canteen is outside smoking a cigarette. She tells me that two people have ordered poached eggs. She says she hates making poached eggs and the thought of having to go back inside to do it is ruining her cigarette break.

A man in an anorak is leaning on his fence smoking a roll-up. He asks me whether I have any mail for him. I tell him I've got to do the estate first and he says he'll hang on for me. An hour-and-a-half later I come off the estate and he's still there, leaning on the fence, smoking a roll-up.

The Border collie has been barking, upsetting ornaments and head-butting the window of the front room of the first house on the cul-de-sac ever since I pushed the mail under the shed door (the owner has asked me not to use the letterbox because the dog tears up the mail). Three doors down, a man in a big quilted coat and aviator shades, winds down the window of his black Honda Prelude with red rims and blacked-out rear windows, winks at me and says "Have you got owt for me mate?" I hand him his mail and he says "Sweet mate. Nice one". At number 12, the large Polish man with the paintbrush moustache who wears his tracksuit bottoms very high (they go right up his arse crack) has been pruning next door's overhanging hypericum with an electric carving knife. Now, he's talking to another neighbour, the young Asian man in the white hooded top who is walking an aggressive looking boxer dog. When I pass them, the dog sees me and nearly pulls him over, jerking him around 180 degrees. The boxer's barking sends the collie at number 2 into a frenzy and it jumps onto the window sill with all four feet, its fur squashed up against the glass. It falls off again in quite a comical fashion but continues to bark undaunted.

Thursday, 24 March

6am: I pass a striking young couple in the town centre. He has a camp lisp, a tight t-shirt, his arms folded and his jeans turned up above the ankle. She is very tall, very blonde and is wearing hot pants and cork wedge sandals. I overhear the man say "I've got to take Sammy's rabbit to get its claws clipped". They head off towards the market place where the stalls are being set up and, a half minute or so later, a chorus of lewd shouts comes up from that direction.

I shout to the woman in the pink turtleneck jumper and grey gilet who is valeting her Peugeot 107 but she can't hear me above Michael Jackson's 'Bad' on the car stereo. When I eventually attract her attention she looks flustered and embarrassed. She apologises and says she's in a world of her own.

The man in the bobble hat and the plastic-rimmed glasses stares as I empty the pillar box. I glance up and let on. He's picking his nose vigorously. He doesn't acknowledge me but continues staring and picking. I carry on clearing the box but I can still feel him staring. I look up again and this time the man glances down quickly and starts to examine the bogey he's been rolling between his thumb and forefinger. I slam the box shut and drag the sack of mail across the pavement. As I load it into the van, the man continues to stare and has now started to excavate the other nostril. He's prodding around up there, tipping his head on one side to get a good purchase and the only time he takes his eyes off me is to inspect the end of his finger. I get into my van just as the man's bus arrives: Stotts…taking people to places.

The garden wall at number 27 is now a pile of rubble after a bus crashed into it the other day. The bus company have erected a 'Temporary Bus Stop' next to it.

The spare wheel cover of the Suzuki Grand Vitara on the driveway at number 47 is decorated with a psychedelic picture of a native American Indian standing next to a rainbow while a large starburst sun rises behind his head like a halo. The car's owner is in his garden wearing nothing but a pair of cut-off denim shorts to strim around the two small whitewashed boulders in the middle of the lawn.

I pass two men on my way home. The first, a man in his fifties, is wearing a heavy long overcoat, a woollen scarf and black leather shoes. The second, a young man in his twenties, wears a t-shirt, knee-length cotton shorts, no socks and flip-flops.

Tuesday, 5 April

There's a brown lace-up Clarks shoe on the pavement outside the house with the ring of miniature standing stones on the lawn. The other of the pair is twenty yards down the road at the bus stop where the chubby goth boy is being chased by a wasp.

Outside Euphoria Fitness, a man and a woman in boxing gloves are sparring in the car-park. He's holding up his hand and she's hitting it. He's shouting "Hit it! Hit it!". I cross the road to the garage where, coincidentally the mechanic is listening to a song with the lyric "euphoria, take my hand" while he works on an old Vauxhall Corsa.

Someone has written 'Lynard Skynard' and 'The Who' in the dirt on my van.

The skip lorries are tailing back down the road from the tip. An elderly man in salwar kameez has climbed into the back of one of them and is raiding it for timber.

Two men are playing pool In the communal room at the flats. One of them is unable to take his preferred shot because his cueing action is obstructed by the still fully decorated Christmas tree in the corner. Outside, I can hear a teacher in the schoolyard opposite shouting "Quickly Shakira, I'm waiting!"

I call round at a friend's house and I notice his neighbour has put up a wobbly, hand-painted sign on his gate that says, 'If you are preaching or selling do not enter coz the wife bites'.

Sunday, 10 April

The man drinking White Star cider on the bench just down from the Shine On Hand Car Wash ('Only One Using Genuine Chamois Leathers') demands

I stroke his bow-legged bull terrier. He promises it won't bite. I stroke its head and it jumps up at my knee, wagging its tail affectionately. The man laughs and says "Told you".

There are three bunches of flowers tied to the branches of the small tree behind The Mahal ('The Only Genuine Charcoal Tandoor (Clay Oven) In Town.') They are still in their cellophane packaging with sachets of flower food attached.

A man with a ginger beard is erecting an authentic looking teepee in unbleached canvas on the grass at the bottom of the flats. Two other men in their thirties are staging a fight with cudgels and large Viking shields. A small group of spectators lines the railings: a teenage couple in tracksuits smoking cigarettes and a man in his late twenties in a tracksuit and a bandana who is sipping beer from a can and fondling his genitals.

The woman who answers the door after the third knock struggles to sign for her parcel while holding a veil over her face at the same time. She's wearing England slippers with a cross of St George motif.

Tuesday, 19 April

The sun has been shining. People are squinting their eyes and shielding the screens of their phones at bus stops. It's hot, I counted seventy-three discarded drinks containers on my way into work this morning. An average of one every thirty-four meters.

Someone has written 'HeRB' on the Church Street post box.

The milkman's two young assistants are talking as they wait on the kerb for the van. "She asked for nine semi, I put twelve in and now she wants thirteen", says the short chubby white one. "Why?" asks the short chubby black one. "Because she's a greedy bitch", says the white one.

The man in the green Atari t-shirt drops the cardboard packaging from his toy machine gun onto the pavement by the bench at the corner of John William Street—where the woman with the short skirt used to feed the pigeons.

Inside the motorcycle showroom, a sales assistant is recommending a bike cleaning product to a customer: "We had a leak from a can of it a while back and when we'd cleaned it up the floor was sparkling! White as snow. Amazing stuff!" "I think I'd better get some of that then", says the customer.

Thursday, 21 April

At the new housing development that now occupies the site of the old mill, the garages are too small to fit cars inside. Consequently, the streets are double lined with mainly silver Puntos and Astras. I brake to avoid a young boy who is staggering from one side of the road to the other while balancing an upside-down yard brush on one finger.

In town, I see Howard from the house on the moor. He waves an envelope at me and says "Bastards have taken £550 off my pension in interest!" He crosses to my side of the street, "There'll be none of that when my lot get in: BNP. We'll string all them bankers up. Bastards! And the bloody unions! They've fucked your pension up, haven't they? Bastards! They've gone fucking soft! In my day if anyone had gone within a mile of our pension fund the union would have had us all out, shut the place down completely. I was out for twelve week once, nearly bloody starved to death. Ended up scotching for a pound an hour. Never told anyone. I had to do it. The unions now are bastards". He jabs me in the chest "They're condemning you to a life of poverty. The bastards!" I say I need to get going and Howard says "I hope you're not rushing round for them bastards. Bastards!"

Friday, 29 April

The tall thin woman with the Highland terrier under her arm says "Oh super, union jack bun cases!" and, under the buddleia in the park, the police are pouring away litre bottles of White Star cider.

Three red-faced, grey-haired men wearing gold, wire-rimmed glasses and sun-bleached anoraks are smoking on the doorstep of the pub. Next door, at the ice-cream parlour, three swishy haired girls in t-shirts and sweatpants sit at a chrome table on the pavement sipping smoothies and eating sorbet.

A young boy of about seven with a cast on his arm tries to get into my van. I shout a warning to him. He says he's looking for his parcel. I say I haven't got a parcel for him and he calls me a dumbo and grabs hold of my arm to see what I'm carrying. The front door of the house opposite opens and a woman calls the boy in. He ignores her and reiterates that he thinks I'm a dumbo. The woman calls him again, twice, but he continues to ignore her and she eventually gives up and goes back inside. I open the door of my van and the boy jumps in. I grab him and drag him out. He's muttering about his parcel and me being a dumbo. When I get into the driver's seat the boy keeps opening my door before I can lock it. In the end, I drive off with it still open. He chases me down the street shouting "Dumbo!"

When I get to the end of Victoria Road, the way is blocked by a long wheelbase van on its side behind a police cordon.

A couple get off the bus. They are each holding a hand of a little boy of about two or three years old. They walk down the street with the boy between them and fail to notice his trousers gradually slipping down to his ankles. The boy struggles to keep up because his movement is restricted. He can't adjust his trousers because the couple are holding his hands. He looks up, trying to make the couple aware of his predicament but they're chatting and don't notice. Eventually, when they are almost having to drag the boy along, they look down. They stop and laugh and the woman adjusts the boy's trousers and gives him a kiss on the cheek.

I catch three teenage boys writing 'Paki's Rule' and 'Pussy' on my garden gate.

Saturday, 7 May

Mr Briggs pulls up, "You'll be getting sunburnt with no cap on", he says. "I'm living on the edge", I say. "Oh", he says, and he drives away, spinning the wheels of his Suzuki Carry in dust by the five bar gate.

There's a copy of *The Watchtower* magazine pinned to the front door of one of the back-to-backs. Someone has scrawled across Jesus' face in biro, "NOT INTERESTED, ONE WORD FREE WILL!"

As we watch the police moving the drunks along in the park, Michael tells me he once saw a man staggering down the street with a bottle in his hand and another two in the pockets of his coat. He said he watched the man's expression turn from horror to relief as the bottle in his hand had slipped onto the floor but hadn't broken. But then, as he bent down to pick it up, the bottles from his pockets fell out and smashed all over the pavement and his expression had turned to one of bewildered anguish.

The swallows are swooping after the flies that buzz around the cow shit on the track down to the farm. I make my way up to the house and knock at the door. The air is fetid and still, hung thick with the stench of pig shit. A woman with a grey bob and plastic-rimmed glasses opens the door. She winces and says "Oh! What a foul smell!" Then, with one hand over her nose, she grabs the parcel from me and shuts the door behind her without saying goodbye.

The man who is brewing beer in his garden and doesn't wear a shirt says hello.

I stand on a dead mouse and, after several minutes of trying, I can't get the worst of it out from the tread of my shoes.

Wednesday, 11 May

The man in the black Astra is blocking the street where he has stopped to answer his phone. He breaks off briefly from his call to wind down his window and shout, "You fat fucking bitch!" to the woman in the red Saab at the front of the queue of oncoming traffic. She doesn't move because she can't; he's blocking the road ahead and she has a queue of traffic behind her. The man calls the Saab woman a fat bitch a couple more times before he finishes his call and then speeds off, shouting "You fat bitch!" a final time as he goes.

Half an hour later I see the man again, he's dropping an old man off at the hospital. They are smiling and sharing a joke together. The man takes the old man's arm and patiently escorts him across the car park and up the steps to the reception area.

At Hill Park, the air is filled with copulating insects, the yelping of lap dogs and the smell of deep fat fryers. A man in jeans is putting a fresh coat of magnolia Wethershield onto his stucco. I say "Good morning" and he makes a sort of "Mgh" noise without looking up.

Garden statues: squirrels, many rabbits, birds (mainly owls and woodpeckers), an elderly couple on a bench, hedgehogs, a donkey (with saddle bags), a horse, an angel, a castle, windmills, otters, a fox, tortoises, cats, highly glazed orbs, a ten foot tall giraffe, ducks, gnomes, Buddhas, frogs (two that croak as I walk past), a miniature Chinese terracotta army figure, some miniature Easter Island heads, fairies, a lion, cats, dogs

(mainly terriers and collies), naked/ semi-naked women, men with golf bags/ cricket bats/shotguns/bags with swag written on them, moulded resin imitation Jean Arp/Barbara Hepworths...

A plane takes off from the airfield. Its engine cuts out for about five seconds as it flies overhead.

Mr Ainley asks me why the mail is so late these days. He says he's going to write to his MP and "sort the bugger out".

Tuesday, 24 May

At the newsagent where the Adele album is played on a loop, two men in their fifties compare their experiences of school. "When the bell rang and we were playing football, we'd just ignore it. Did you do that?" says one. "No, not really" says the other.

On Bankfoot Lane, a man in a flat cap is clearing debris left by the high winds. He holds up a garden gnome, "I just found this", he says "Isn't he a little beauty?"

I get hit in the face by a wet clematis when it breaks free of its trellis in a strong gust and a woman answers her door wearing a Father Christmas oven glove. Also, the Christmas tree is still up and fully decorated in the pool room at the flats.

I see an owl at Wheelwright's farm, a young boy of about seven threatens to cut my head off with an axe and the man in the park with a chest-length beard and Bermuda shorts asks me whether I've ever been to London.

I see Marc getting off the bus at Berry Brow. He has a snare drum in one hand, some cymbals in the other and his jacket is done up to the top. I pull over to say hello and he says he's just got back from London where he's played at Ronnie Scott's. I say to say hello to his mum, he says he will and then he sets off home because it starts raining.

Friday, 27 May

I still pass the man with the tartan Thermos and the all-year-round woolly hat on my way into work but I've stopped saying hello since it obviously makes him so uncomfortable. This morning I happened to glance up as he approached and he faked a trip to avoid making eye contact.

I deliver a parcel to a man with a side parting and a plaid shirt. He tells me it's a box of chocolates. He suggests that should I ever want to get round the wife then I could do worse than to order some myself. "They really are first class", he says, "far more effective than flowers". The man also mentions that he owns a Volvo V70 which he also recommends very highly, "A beautiful car" he says.

The man whose shirt is perforated with tiny hot rock holes apologises for his signature. "It's gone a bit funny", he says.

Wildlife of note: two dead hedgehogs, one dead blackbird, one dead squirrel, one heron (alive), one woodpecker (alive).

Thursday, 2 June

Up the driveway of replica stone setts, past the box trees, the cobbles, the blue slate chippings and the saplings with their nursery tags flapping in the breeze to the faux timber door. A large cockchafer has turned turtle on the doorstep. I right it gently with the toe end of my boot.

Twice in succession during my parcel delivery, the door is answered by a middle-aged woman with a broken arm.

At the next house, the door is answered by a man in his thirties with shaving foam all over his chin. Another full hour into the delivery and somebody else with a broken arm answers a door. This time it's a middle-aged man, his sweater bulging over the bad arm with the empty sleeve dangling at his side.

The man with the regulation haircut and the 4x4 in the carpark of the gym explains how much he hates show muscle. "All the young lads are into it", he says. "They look good but they've got no stamina. I was sparring with a lad twice my size and half my age yesterday and I just hung in there till he wore himself out and then gave him a good smack in the kidneys."

A grey wagtail flits around in the dust on the forecourt of the BMW garage. I go inside through the big glass doors and when I hand over the package to the man in the blue overalls, he says "Is it a food parcel from UNICEF?" I laugh but when the overall man looks for a reaction from the man at the desk in the corner— crew neck sweater with his shirt collar tucked inside—he doesn't get one.

Tuesday, 7 June

6am: Three men are playing on the roundabout in the children's playground.

The one with the black bandana tied around his head is pushing it round as fast as he can and repeatedly shouting "Oh baby! You're gonna die!"

A man in military uniform carries a carriage clock across Church Street.

At the newsagent's, Christine is on the till. She tells me the new owner is applying for an off-license. "I don't want to be in here on my own at ten o' clock at night with all the skanks coming in. It's a local newsagent for goodness sake, he thinks he's bloody Tesco's."

A man in sportswear watches me deliver a parcel. He's leaning on a broken fence with a bottle of Ribena in one hand and his bollocks in the other.

A woman walks past the pink teddy bear in the road on her way up to Dead Man's Hole. She's wearing a pale grey fleece jacket, black ski-pants and she's carrying a shopping bag that's so big she's holding it with her arm bent at the elbow so it doesn't drag along the floor. She's talking on a phone: "Joan has been up with some boxes and one looked like it might have been a cat basket".

I find a four leaf clover in Dead Man's Hole.

Adam Ant's tour bus is parked outside Holmfirth Post Office.

Things people said to me today after I handed them their post (not including 'Thank you' or variations thereof which is what most people say): "Is that it? That's a poor do." "Ooh, lots!" "That's not too bad." "That's great." "Parcel? Oh yes, that's David's tea actually, birdseed." "You haven't been knocking long have you? I was asleep." "Oh my God!"

Saturday, 11 June

Yesterday, I saw a crow pick up a basket-ball-sized piece of scrunched up fish and chip paper in its beak and fly away over the houses with it. Later, on the same street, I saw a woman in a spangly lilac sari and headscarf hoovering the pavement outside her house with big upright Dyson.

Earlier today, I was smoking on the steps at the entrance to the park opposite the post office with Michael. I told him about the woman I'd seen hoovering the pavement and he told me he'd once seen a man watering his garden despite the fact he'd paved over it several years earlier. I suggested that the man might simply have been cleaning his flags, but Michael said that when he'd asked him what he was doing, the man had said he was watering the flowers. At this point in the conversation, a sparrow flew down and landed in the gap between us on the step, about two feet away from each of us. Michael didn't notice so I caught his eye, said, "Aye-up, who's this?" and I glanced down at the bird. When Michael caught sight of it, he started with a small yelp of surprise.

The sparrow flew off and Michael said: "I fucking hate birds".

A group of school children pass me in the street. They all have their coats over their heads to block the glare of the sun on their phone screens.

Sunday, 19 June

I walk into work in the slipstream of a man who is smoking strong weed and listening to Chaka Demus and Pliers without headphones. As we walk through the Market Place, a splay-footed drunkard wearing the remains of a tuxedo shouts "HELLO!" to us both from the steps of Headrow Furnishers.

Two women in their seventies are discussing custard tart: "It was lovely, I had the custard tart", says the tallish one with the mid-calf length floral-print pleated skirt and the Summer Wine perm. "Ooh, I do love custard tart", says the shortish one with the mid-calf length floral-print pleated skirt and the Summer Wine perm. "My mother used to make the best custard tart—lovely thin pastry." Says the tallish one. "Lovely. My husband says he doesn't care how thick the pastry is!" Says the shortish one, eyebrows outraged. "Well, that's it you see: men don't mind so much about the pastry. All they're interested in is the custard. All men love custard." "That's true. Whenever we go anywhere the men always go for the custard option. It's a schoolboy thing I think." "You're right."

At the house with the balloons tied to the gate posts, the builders are swearing on the roof. I count seven "fuckings" and a "bastard" in the time it takes for the young mum to walk her two toddlers up the driveway to the front door for the birthday party.

Sunday, 3 July

Mr Barton has fixed a hook adjacent to his back door on which he hangs the fully loaded super-soaker he uses to dissuade cats from fouling his borders. He has also been shooting squirrels with an air rifle. I've counted seven dead in his back garden in the last few days. When I asked him about it earlier in the week he claimed they'd all died of old age but yesterday he admitted to having shot them. He said, "They don't understand death like we do", and he made a fist with his right hand and beat his chest above his heart, "We are the only ones who know we're going to die".

On the other side of the road, a hefty teen girl with dyed red hair, black satin tracksuit top, black tights, black jersey mini-skirt, and a pair of disintegrating grey Ugg boots was violently shoving a spotty teen boy outside the newsagent's shop, "You gave me one-pound-fucking-twenty. Fuck off!" she yelled.

Saturday, 9 July

5.30am: I pass a house from which the theme tune from the TV show *Countdown* is blaring. A police helicopter hovers directly overhead.

A colleague tells me he'd been embarrassed the other day while delivering a package to a sex shop on his round; he tripped up a step and knocked over a display of dildos.

At the house with the decorative Father Christmas and snowman figurine in the window, I hand the owner a parcel. He's an elderly man dressed almost entirely in a single hue of beige (he would probably appear to be naked from a distance). He shouts to me above the noise of his dog barking from behind the gate, "Don't worry!" he says, "She's all this" and he makes a C-shaped gesture with his right hand, opening and closing his thumb and fingers to signify talking. "Just like all women", he adds with a wink.

I knock at the door of the house in Manor Street where the owner always jokes that his parcels are consignments

of heroin. Littering his short garden path are twenty-nine cigarette butts, fifty-seven KFC salt sachets (some opened and some unopened), a KFC vinegar sachet (unopened), a drinking straw and an empty litre and a half bottle of Fanta. There are also a lot of white feathers—far too many to count.

While using the urinal in the toilets on the first floor of the post office, I glance out of the open window and notice a shoe on top of the security hut at the main entrance. It's one of those chisel-toe slip-ons with a three-quarter inch heel.

Thursday, 14 July

5.30am: A man who can't walk straight passes me on the other side of the road. He's wearing plastic-rimmed glasses and carrying a copy of *The Guardian* under his arm. He staggers slightly, bounces off the wall with his shoulder and spills Pepsi Max down his top.

In the park, a dozen or so people are playing loud music in the bandstand. They wave and shout "Morning, mate!" as I pass. When I reply they all collapse in fits of laughter.

I was emptying a postbox when the man in the garden behind it threw a large snail over his shoulder without looking. It bounced off the side of my head and set off across the road with half its shell missing.

Later, on Mayfield Avenue, a woman opened the window of her front room and asked me to help her and her husband to climb out. She said they'd locked themselves in.

Out of the five people inside the motorcycle showroom, I am the only one without grey hair and a moustache. I go over to the counter where a grey-haired man with a moustache breaks off briefly from his conversation ("She makes a lovely sound, especially when you open her up a bit") to tell me that I am "looking for parts" (which I'm not) He points

to an adjoining door and says "Through there, mate. They'll look after you".

The signs to the car-park at the enormous new church say 'Customer Parking'.

Sunday, 24 July

6.00am: As I walk down Fitzwilliam Street, a gust of wind blows an empty Tennent's Super can from the gutter and it begins to roll noisily across the street. When It reaches the middle of the road, it changes course and starts a descent down the hill at quite a speed. I watch as it overtakes me. About twenty yards further down, a rat appears from the opposite pavement and begins to scuttle across the road on a collision course with the can at the intersection of their paths. I wait for the crash, which seems inevitable, but the rat puts on an impressive turn of speed at the last second and disappears into Marco's Hand Car Wash unimpeded.

I apologise to the man at the County Court for the temperamental nature of my PDA when it shuts down as he's about to sign for the mail. "It reminds me of a woman", he says. Outside, in the car park, two women in tears console each other next to a Vauxhall Corsa.

The university is busy with graduates in mortar boards and gowns. I queue to get into the car park behind a red Ferrari with the number plate G1RLS.

There are two identical settee cushions — brown with a bit of white stuffing poking out—in the road at either end of Newsome Avenue.

In St Peter's Street someone has stuck a penny to the side of a bin with a blob of gob and a bit further down there are three short blue pencils fastened to the back of the pay and display machine with masking tape.

A woman in a maxi dress is painting a shed while listening to Take That in the gardens next to the art gallery.

Saturday, 28 January 2012

Outside the flats, two men in their late sixties wearing fleece jackets and woolly hats, are discussing RSJs, purlins and caustic soda. They are with a woman of a similar age. She is wearing large spectacles, red lipstick, and a well-padded, snug-fitting gilet.

A tall man with a shaved head stops me in the street and says, "Have you noticed them?" He frees up his right hand by consolidating all his Argos bags into his left, and points at the sky. "What?" I say. "Them", says the man, and points again. "The vapour trails?" I say. "Yes. They're not normal", he says. "Look at them. Look at the crisscrossing and the angle. They shouldn't be at that angle." The man lines up his hand with one of the plumy trails, squinting across it with one eye closed to get a more accurate gauge. "They shouldn't dissipate like that either. I've been doing some research: these aren't civilian planes doing this, they are military. I've got software that tells me where all your British Airways, Virgin, Ryanair… all the Manchester airport stuff should be, but these planes never show up. I've noticed them a lot over Huddersfield recently." "What are they doing?" I ask. "Spraying chemicals", he says. "What for?" "I don't know. If I told you what I think they're doing it for, you'd think I was some kind of nutter." He smiles and re-distributes his Argos bags. He tells me he can't say any more because he has to go, and he legs it across the street shouting: "Just look up Chemtrails on Google! See you, mate!"

At the house on the moor, Howard holds up a letter to show me. Printed on the envelope it says: 'Give Blood—Donor Survey'. Howard lowers his brow and growls "Survey, my arse! I'll give 'em a bloody survey through the sights of my bloody rifle!" On the way out of the yard, I slip on a frozen pool of dog piss.

Birds: Jay, Buzzard, Treecreeper, heron, pheasants.

Monday, 6 February

There's a dead long-tailed tit on the step of the house where the woman says she's not quite dressed yet.

The two women in fleece jackets and black tracksuit bottoms with white trim are jogging in opposite directions along Station Road. They don't acknowledge one another as they pass.

The woman at the bus stop tells me her oven has blown up. She says she had glass in her hair and was having to use her grill instead which was doing her head in.

Sunday, 12 February

Out on a rural delivery among the suggestive trees, where the glass re-cyclers are full of wine bottles rather than greasy pasta sauce jars, a woman with large spectacles and red lipstick says it's a glorious day as she wipes her hands on her pinny. There are lapwings, fieldfares, a moorhen, a buzzard, three plastic herons and two dozen bottles of Budweiser chilling in the snow by the back door. The receptionist lifts her half-rimmed specs and confides that the security officer is "a right twat" and later, in the bright midday sun, a man with a switched-on lamp attached to a headband pulls up in a Ford Focus and says "Those vans are breeding, there's another one down there".

Dave Robertson is singing a medley of his improvised lyrics to classic tunes in the yard again. To the tune of 'Panic' by The Smiths: "Panic on the streets of Sheepridge. Where's me Giro? Where's me Giro? Where's me Giro?" To the theme of *Last of the Summer Wine*: "I love my job, I need to see a psychiatrist" and to the tune of Bob Marley's 'No Woman, No Cry': "No money, no beer".

Saturday, 18 February

The man opposite me on the bus keeps gesturing towards me and saying "This postman, he is lost" in a fake eastern European accent. After a while, his companion joins in too: "These sex toys are not for me, the brothel is not open yet". They are both finding this very amusing.

On the pavement below the pub chalkboard advertising a concert by a band called Rockweiler, there is a pillow in a clean white case.

At the houses where they have removed the Yorkstone flags from the paths and replaced them with old Nurishment drink cans, empty Space Raiders/Jelly Tots/Tesco bags, extrusions of expanding foam, splinters of 4x2 timber, fake patent snakeskin handbags with broken handles, pairs of black tracksuit bottoms with white trim, faded-plastic children's ride-on cars with broken wheels, milk cartons, dog shit, old carpet griprods and empty lager cans, I disturb a would-be burglar. He runs away up the cobbles wearing black tracksuit bottoms with white trim and a hooded top.

The Polish man at number 131 who gets all the parcels is wearing some new BMW slippers.

There are seventeen separate piles of dog shit in the six square metres of concreted-over yard at number 85. Around the corner, the man with the shaved head who lives at number 81 is pissing in the middle of the street outside his house while his partner struggles to get their toddler down the front steps in a pushchair.

As I lift open the broken gate of the house with 'PRIVT NO PARKING PLS' written on it in foot-high white letters, the front door opens suddenly and somebody hurls two fully loaded nappy bags roughly in the direction of the overflowing wheelie bins on the pavement. They miss me, and the bins, by about a metre.

Tuesday, 28 February

It's getting light as I walk through the park. Two Border collies are rounding up the ducks while a woman in a sky blue anorak and bleached hair shouts at them to stop.

The man who has the look of a comedy vicar from the 1970s is repairing a dry stone wall. He tries to wave as I pass but he can't lift up his arm because he's holding a large piece of stone.

"Oh no! No way! I don't talk to her!" says the big woman with the grey regulation buzz cut and the unusually large black plastic rimmed glasses when I ask her whether she'd mind taking in a parcel for her neighbour. She lets out her black Labradors and they bark at me through the wire fence that divides the gardens—rough lawns, rockeries and garden centre ornamentation. Then, a huge man of girth and height who is dressed for sport in brown boots, moleskins and a shooting vest, comes out and loads the dogs into an old metallic grey 4x4 and drives them away in the direction of the moor.

The crisp packet in the road wasn't a pheasant as I'd thought, it was a crisp packet.

On the moor, I watch a crow seeing off a kestrel while Mr Anderson buzzes around his topiary armchair with a noisy hedge trimmer. On the edge of the wood, I see a jay and a bullfinch.

On the doorstep of the Manor House, someone has arranged a small display of those smooth grey pebbles with the white calcite stripes through them. Back in town, I notice Mrs Haigh has hung a canvas print of similar pebbles above the coal effect fireplace and the wood effect laminate floor.

Saturday, 3 March

Tony gives me a lift to work in his new car. It has a de-mister that comes on when he literally tells it too. I tell Julie about it and she says Tony has five sugars in his tea.

This week's wildlife of note: a woodpecker, a jay, some lapwings, a lark, rabbits, deer, a dead fox, some chickens, up to two dozen black Labradors, numerous koi carp and two plastic herons (one standing up and one lying down on its side).

The chickens at the farm peck at the dog's bone while the builders listen to 'People Are People' by Depeche Mode on their heavy duty site radio.

I couldn't get up to Hill Top because of the two rival dog walkers' vans that had parked to collect their charges from houses on opposite sides of the street.

Mr Briggs pulls up to tell me he's just heard on the news that the cheapest petrol station in town is the Jet garage at Lockwood.

The woman in the trench coat asks "Is it going to make a nice day, do you think?" "I'm not sure but it's looking good at the minute" I reply. "I know, but will it last?" says the woman.

Thursday, 15 March

On my way into work, I pass a man I often see around. He never speaks to me but he once held open the door at the Co-op and he sometimes nods stiffly in my direction. On this occasion though, he ignores me completely.

The chubby man with the comb-over is in the park, he's with his black Labrador, John.

A man with tippie-tappie winklepicker shoes and a Liverpool FC plastic carrier bag passes me on the pavement as a Suzuki Swift kills a pigeon at the traffic lights.

On the estate of barely detached houses with the mainly black high-performance German cars. I call at number 3 where

the mini with 'Maureen' written on it is parked in the driveway. I wait on the front step next to a scale model of a baby rabbit and the doormat which has 'NICE TO SEE YOU, TO SEE YOU NICE' written on it. Next door, a man in a suit and dark glasses pauses before unlocking the door of his BMW. He glances over at me across his plastic lawn and says, "Anything for numero uno before I head off?" I say there isn't. Eventually, the door of number 3 opens and a thin man in his sixties wearing a dressing gown undone to the waist smiles and says "Good morning, sir!" I smile back and hand him his package "Yes. Thank you! Thanks a lot. Ta. Thank you. Thank you" he says.

Also today: some men playing the bagpipes on the ring-road and an owl.

Friday, 23 March

There's nobody around apart from three men in hi-visibility clothing—myself being one of them. I'm in orange, the others in green. We each walk down different streets towards their confluence which we reach simultaneously.

I've seen the man in the all-year-round head-to-toe waterproofs twice today. The first time he was running up Heaton Road with his waterproof hood up, then I saw him again with his hood down. He appeared to be giving directions to somebody in a Kia Rio on Outcote Bank.

A man in his thirties was standing in the road talking to an elderly woman. She was wearing beige salwaar kameez, headscarf, thick plastic rimmed glasses and a pair of black canvas pumps with a white skull and crossbones motif. The man had a dog, a huge Akita, which was also in the road, as was another man who, with his buck teeth and moustache had a look of Freddie Mercury about him. It was this man who was encouraging

the four children of between about six and nine years to pelt the dog with sticks and small stones from a distance of about two metres. The dog's owner and the woman were both aware of what was happening but did nothing to discourage the children as missiles began to pile up around their feet. The dog was placid, reacting only to duck between its owner and the old woman for shelter when the barrage became particularly intense. The children continued to throw stuff while Freddie Mercury sourced ammunition for them. Eventually, I got into my van and pulled out from the kerb. None of the children, the two men, the woman or the dog attempted to get out of my way and I sat waiting for about thirty seconds. Finally, the man pulled his dog onto the kerb and out of range of the children who then retreated to the other side so I could pass, crushing piles of sticks and pebbles under the wheels as I went.

Saturday, 31 March

My neighbour keeps free-range rabbits, chickens and guinea fowl. She lives in a terraced house on a busy road with a small, paved yard. She often leaves the gate open so the animals can roam up and down the street. The first time I saw this, I assumed the animals had escaped and I knocked at her door to tell her. She waved me away and told me it didn't matter. This morning a fox was chasing one of her rabbits round and round the house opposite.

I thought I was ten minutes late leaving for work, but I saw all the regulars in their usual places: the black VW Golf with the Polish plates, the silver Punto whose driver sits talking on the phone with the engine running next to the wall where all the pointing fell out in one piece after the bad frost, the 302 bus with the men in hi-vis jackets on board, the tall man who never says hello with his brace of Labradoodles, the woman whose collies round up the ducks in the park, the former postman and his wife who say they couldn't wish for a better lifestyle now he's retired, the brazen blackbird that hops along at my feet for several yards at the entrance to the park, the disheveled starey-eyed beard-on/beard-off man with the jittery gait and his dubiously sourced early morning takeaway. Five Canada geese also fly low over my head in formation on their way to the pond in the park.

The car park attendant has taken to wearing a stab vest.

At the reception of the university halls of residence, the Mike Posner song 'You Think You're Cooler Than Me' is on the radio. Mr Hewitson is on the front desk and when I ask him for his name for the third time this week, I hear the lyric, "…and you never say hey, or remember my name. It's probably cuz, you think you're cooler than me". If Mr Hewitson noticed, he never let on.

At the junior school office, I join the queue behind a woman with a budgerigar in her handbag and a man who is dropping off his daughter while wearing a 'Keep Calm and Eat Pussy' t-shirt.

On my way home, I stop at the supermarket where a fat man in a Spanish football shirt farts loudly by the turnips.

Wednesday, 18 April

I'm a few paces behind beard-on/beard-off man when he drops a ten pence piece on the floor. He bends down to pick it up, cradling his dubiously sourced early morning takeaway to his chest. I overtake him, I round the corner where the market traders are arguing about their pitches and see my boss jogging across the road to the office twenty yards ahead. As he reaches the pavement by the junction box with the 'Oi Ain't Red' sticker on it, he too drops some money and then scrabbles around on the floor to pick it up.

A man in black tracksuit bottoms with white trim tells me to fuck off when he realises I heard him talking to himself.

A jogger with an iPod and a lightweight wind-cheater passes me as I approach the house with the big Audi on the drive and the plastic snowdrops in three miniature galvanised buckets on the doorstep. I'm about to knock at the door when the owner, a woman wearing a black quilted jacket, pulls onto the drive in a new Mini. "How's that for timing?" She says as she gets out of the car. I suggest she must have some kind of sixth sense that tells her when the post is going to arrive and she says "Yep, I'm psychedelic me".

Friday, 18 May

There's a pair of soiled boxer shorts and two smashed Stella bottles on the pavement next to the junction box with 'Kate is gay' written on it.

At the bus station, a group discussion is underway about sandwich filling preferences. The large woman in her fifties says she could never eat peanut butter and cucumber because she doesn't like "sweet and sour stuff".

10am: I find a pair of glasses in the street, thick old lady ones in a leather case. I knock at a nearby house to see if somebody might recognise them, but there's no reply. I try the house next door. There's nobody there either. I cross to the house opposite and walk up the driveway past the caravan with the punctured leather football stuffed over the tow bar. I can see through the window of the front room and behind the display of beer steins on the window sill, there's a man on a settee with the television on. I knock on the door but the man doesn't move. I ring the bell and knock again, harder; he still didn't move. I go to knock on the window but as I get closer I realise the man is asleep. I don't wake him up, I go next door, where I can see another man sitting in front of a television. I knock at his door and, once again, the man doesn't move; he is asleep as well. Eventually, a further two doors down, somebody answers: a woman with short grey hair and a beige fleece. She takes the glasses from me and says she thinks they belong to a neighbour. "I bet she'll have dropped them on the way to the bus stop. She'll have grabbed something out of her bag…" says the woman, twisting around and miming grabbing something from an imaginary bag, "…she'll have yanked at it and pulled her glasses out by mistake. Thanks love, I'll bob over with them when she gets back".

Down the road from where Dik got a nail in his foot, next to the yellow grit bin that's overgrown with nettles, an elderly couple waits for me to pull up in my van. The man is wearing head-to-toe beige and the woman, head-to-toe pale lavender. Both wear Reactolite glasses which are in full anti-glare bloom. "Anything exciting for us!" shouts the lavender lady as I get out. "No. Next door" I say. "You want to get a coat", says the man "They're very good those fleeces but they don't keep out the rain!"

According to the poster sellotaped to the lamp-post, the cat with the bit of tinsel around its neck is still missing.

Monday, 28 May

I knock at the door. Nobody comes. While I wait, a man in a blue suit walks past in the street, "Carry it out within the usual framework…" he says into his phone. I knock at the door again but nobody answers so I go to the next house along where I see a woman in the front room watching the television. I knock and rang the bell but the woman doesn't come. I knock again. She still doesn't come. As I make my way back to the first house to leave a note, I glance up to see whether the woman is still watching the television. She's not; she's standing with her back against the wall in the lee of the chimney breast, head turned away, trying to be invisible.

A man wearing shorts and a Superman t-shirt that is too small for him has stopped to talk to a woman in the street. "Honestly," says the woman, "she's such a weirdo, she just phoned me and said 'I just had to pick up a dead pigeon. What are you up to?'"

Sunday, 3 June

At the house with the sign on the gate that says 'My Doberman lives here' above a picture of a Doberman's head and a human hand holding a torch, I stand on a snail as a helicopter flies overhead. On the window sill with the dead moths, there is a money tree plant, a single white sock, a dusty snooker trophy and a TDK D90 audio cassette— still in its packaging. When I knock at the door, a man with tattoo sleeves answers, "It's awkward when you can't see your own writing", he says as he fills in his signature.

I call at a house with a parcel but nobody is home. I notice people at the house next door so I go to ask whether they'll take the parcel for their neighbour. A young man in a vest and jogging pants answers. He agrees to take the parcel and asks, "Are they trainers?" I say I don't know. "I might try them on", he says. He winks at me and then he puts his hand down the front of his trousers, adjusts his cock and shuts the door.

Two men are talking on the bus: "Have you ever murdered anyone, Carl?" "No, I haven't, Jim." "No, me neither."

A snail crawls up my kitchen window on the morning of the diamond jubilee of HRH Queen Elizabeth ll.

Friday, 15 June

I pull up too far from the control unit for the entry barrier at the entrance to the technical college. There's a queue of traffic behind me so I can't manoeuvre

the van any closer. I open my door and stretch out my arm as far as I can but my foot gets tangled in the mat in the footwell and I fall out onto the road.

Today's dead wildlife: a frog, a shrew, a slug, two snails, a bee, a squirrel, two earthworms, a wasp, half a starling, and a large moth (the moth was inside a packet of Coco-Pops).

The woman with the new BMW and the tight jeans tells her neighbour, a man in cargo pants and a white t-shirt, "When you only pay two, three, four grand for a car it's gonna be a heap of shit". "I know", says the man, "There was no heated seat, no CD player nor nowt!"

The woman at one of the barn conversions on the moor has pressed her old aerobics step into use as a stand to display her houseplants on. She has created a two-tiered tableau in the big picture window at the front that looks out onto her neighbour's Mitsubishi Animal. Next door, where the garden backs onto acres of idyllic rolling countryside as far as the eye can see, Mrs Moorhouse pedals determinedly on the exercise bike she's rigged up in her garage.

Two window cleaners talk as they drip suds from their Suzuki Carry to the houses on the estate. "They were good sarnies this morning, you know", says the smaller, younger of the two who is carrying a bucket and some ladders. "I still would rather have had a breakfast", says the bigger, older one who is carrying the van keys. "I know what you're saying", says the younger one.

Tuesday, 26 June

At 6am my neighbour slams his front door and shouts "Bastard!" at the top of his voice.

At 6.30am two young women lie on their backs in the middle of the Northumberland Street, singing.

At 12.20pm in Victoria Road, the man in the heavy beige anorak in 23°C wears two Mansize tissues under the arms of his glasses like large white blinkers.

At 2.30pm at the farm, the barbed wire fence is hung with clumps of snagged wool, the horse wearing the blanket kicks the one that isn't in the face and the two Border terriers bark hysterically, almost throttling themselves on their chains. A swallow flies low over a dry stone wall, skilfully avoiding a collision with the giant fat ceramic blue tit which is fastened to the top of the gate post with a big blob of cement. Also, the farmer has just told me that his neighbour is a lazy cunt.

Wednesday, 4 July

I was walking past the newsagent's shop when somebody threw a slimy mango stone out of a first-floor window. It landed where I was just about to step. I adjusted my stride to the left to avoid it

but the stone bounced and my foot came down right on top of it. I slipped on the stone but managed to retain my balance.

The builder with the swagger and the four-foot spirit level calls me boss and tells me his dog doesn't like postmen. I approach the front door of the house he's working on and the dog barks threateningly, its hair on end. The builder ignores the situation and climbs some scaffolding singing the Howard Jones song 'Like To Get To Know You Well'. The owner of the house has to come out and collect his mail from me.

An old man with no teeth wheels a broken swivel chair out to his bins. "Nothing lasts forever!" he says.

Sunday, 15 July

The UPVC door opens and a man wearing a blue fleece jacket and a large rucksack over a black pin-striped suit steps out. He stands between the two lilies in plastic terracotta pots to lock up, then turns and walks towards me. "This weather looks a bit naughty!" he says as he passes, looking up at the sky, "And they say it's gonna get worse an' all".

'Horny' by Mousse T is playing over the PA in the toyshop. Down the road, the secretary at the recruitment agency says her signature makes her look like "a right spaz", and later, at the chemical plant, the security guard confiscates my lighter before he lets me on site. He's chewing gum ferociously but his breath still smells strongly of alcohol.

I follow a large hare for about fifty yards as it bounds along in the middle of the road. It darts off into the field where the magic mushrooms grow in the autumn.

I pass the woman in the beige three-quarter length anorak with all the ties pulled as tight as possible; only her squashed face is visible under her shiny wet hood, giving her the look of a pantomime maggot. I comment on the miserable weather and she agrees it is disappointing for the time of year. "I heard something funny the other day though." She says. "Oh, it did make me laugh!" She stifles a laugh at the very thought, and explains: "My friend's son says that if the weather carries on like this, we'll be sunbathing on Christmas day!" She throws up her arms, "Oh, I did laugh!" She cackles.

Tuesday, 24 July

A dozen or so young women wearing ponytails and predominantly black lycra with an accent of either cerise pink, cobalt blue, orange, lime green etc are taking part in an outdoor aerobics class in the park. At the bus stop opposite, an elderly woman in a beige anorak arrives and says to the other elderly woman in a beige anorak, "It's been a bit of a rush but I'm here now and that's all that matters".

In the farm shop car park, a woman in a beige anorak tells a man in a beige anorak that she can't get anything except Radio 2 on her car stereo. "Still?" says the old man, rolling his eyes. The woman nods, "I know! After all this time". The man waves a walking stick towards the shop entrance and says, "It's a bit of a walk down there." "I'll go", says the woman, "What do you want?" "A lettuce", says the man.

A heron flies over Shangri-La, a blackbird picks up a sun-baked slug and bounces it on the driveway at Orchard House and, at Greenside, where the man with the pickaxe says he'll be okay as long as it stays dry, a robin is eating some shat-out berries on top of a gate post.

Ernest says his new puppy hasn't been a bit of bother.

Friday, 27 July

The man in his sixties with the faded 'Just Beachin' t-shirt that features a picture of a kitten on a sun lounger is showing a neighbour, another man in his sixties—who has a half-sized resin statue of a horse tethered to his house—around his new car. He points out something on the dashboard, "It's guaranteed for life, that. Mind you, I've heard that before", he says, before pausing to greet the two men in green high-vis vests who are walking past. "Hiya lads", he says with a small wave. "Ayup", says the tallest of the hi-vis men, a pair of long ladders balanced on his shoulder. The other, slimmer and older with grey hair, just nods and smiles; he is carrying a plate of cupcakes decorated with blue butter icing and little silver balls.

I stop to talk to a woman with very straight hair, glasses and a large canvas shopping bag about the problems she's been having moderating her body temperature since the hospital put her on Warfarin. She's concerned her fleece jacket might make her too hot on her way to the bus stop, even though she's taken out the lining. Quite a fat man passes us, he's walking a very small poodle and picking his nose and eating it.

The woman with the dyed black perm and the wind-cheater is talking to the woman in the large 1980s Reactolites. She says she's all fired up about her fish tank again. "It's not been the same since my big shark died. I lost all my enthusiasm, but I've been busy with it again recently…" She breaks off and grabs the Reactolite woman by the arm, "You'll have to come over when the dark nights come back, it looks magical!"

Wednesday, 22 August

The sun is out and the streets are filled with girls in leggings, texting.

At the first house I go to, the garden gate falls off in my hand, at the second, the weight of the opened gate pulls its post from its mounting and, at the third, the flap of the letter-box falls off and lands in the cat's drinking water.

A military veteran in a blazer and a drunk in a matted fleece jacket are at the bus stop. They both have the same style long grey beard and moustache. At the next bus stop, a young man in a hooded top is pretending to fight with the metal post that displays the timetables.

An old VW Golf clanks noisily around the corner. The rear seats are folded down and the load space is packed with rubble and broken bits of wooden pallet, the weight of which has lowered the car's suspension. The car pulls over and a young couple get out. He hands her his on-backwards snapback and she holds onto it as he slides himself underneath the car to locate the noise.

I empty a post box. Next to me, on the pavement, a woman with a striped tracksuit top and a bag-for-life is discussing the price of travel with a large man in a mac, "It's free to Haworth on the bus and I enjoy the journey; it's £20 to Blackburn on the train!" I slam the door of the box shut as a man in a white

Transit van comes around the corner shouting at us all: "Get out my bloody way! Go on!"

I've walked through two spiders' webs today.

Sunday, 2 September

6.00am: I follow the man with the pink Winnie the Pooh duvet wrapped around his shoulders down Heaton Road.

On Fitzwilliam Street, where the Kia Shuma with "Driven by one seriously mad bitch" written across its boot usually parks, I pass two young men in hooded tops. They are in animated conversation, relating to one another their parts in a violent altercation.

Arranged on the pavement outside the roller-shutter doors of the open market are six candles burning in highball glasses where a victim of the "mass brawl!" on Bank Holiday Monday was found.

On the bus, I'd assumed the old woman next to me was talking to herself, but it turned out she was commenting on the weather to me. I apologised and agreed that it had felt a bit cooler of late. Suddenly, the man wearing the tracksuit and holding a half-length mirror a few seats in front of us started ranting at nobody in particular. Most of what he was shouting was incoherent, but the phrases "Make an appointment to see yourself!" and "Have a fucking word with yourself!" were conspicuous. I exchanged a glance with the old woman and she raised her eyebrows and bit her bottom lip. When the man got off a few stops later, the old woman said she'd seen it all now.

Thursday, 13 September

I pass three piles of vomit on my way into work.

I follow a man carrying an overloaded Sainsbury's bag into town. At the

bottom of Fitzwilliam Street, he wanders into the middle of the road and stoops to inspect a discarded Richmond Superkings packet. When he realises it's empty, he boots it across the road and continues on his way, rounding the corner under the railway bridge. As the Superkings man disappears from view, beard-on-beard-off man appears, striding purposefully in the opposite direction while making a noise like a sheep.

I pass an old classmate in the street. I haven't seen him for about twenty years. "Hi, how are you doing?" I say, reaching out to shake his hand. "Not so bad" he says, and he pulls on his cigarette and carries on walking.

Outside the school, the PE class are on a cross-country run. The sturdily built teacher with her hair in a bun and white polo shirt tucked into black tracksuit trousers is berating the half a dozen chubby stragglers: "Power walk, c'mon! Put your arms into it! POWER WALK!"

A white Transit van pulls up next me. The driver leans across and winds down the window, "Mate!" he yells, "Which way is it back to where I just was?"

The man at the terrace on the moor has sprayed his letterbox gold in honour of the Olympics. I post his mail and, as I turn to walk back up the path, a sparrow flies into the back of my leg.

It's been a good few years since the last one, but I saw another headless pigeon corpse today.

Sunday, 23 September

Two black Labradors bark at each other from opposite sides of the street while their owners conduct a loud conversation about black Labradors above the noise.

On the way up to the manor house, I disturbed a heron. I'd thought it was one of those plastic ones until it flapped around in a panic and took off. As I walked back down the drive, I heard a

rustling noise in the trees above me. I looked up in time to avoid a squirrel as it lost its grip and fell, landing with a surprisingly load slap on the tarmac. Startled, it looked up at me, then set off quickly across the lawn.

At the Lodge, the dog has shat in its food bowl.

A man in a white transit van with a sheep's skull fastened to its radiator and a crude depiction of an ejaculating penis in the dirt across its back doors stops to ask me for directions to the farm. I tell him to turn right just after Greengates, "You can't miss it", I say, "it's got massive green gates".

When I arrive at Greengates myself, a half hour or so later, the distinctive gates have gone, replaced by some temporary safety barriers. I ask the owner what has happened. "They're in the garage", he says, "It's been so wet recently, I took them off for re-painting to give the gardeners something to do. Otherwise, they'll sit around drinking fucking tea all day".

On my way home, I called in at the shop. Two young women came in after me, followed by a short man in a shiny old bomber jacket. I took my things to the man at the till—the Asian one with the greying bob and pencil moustache—and, as he checked out my stuff, the bomber jacket man walked behind me and out of the shop without buying anything. The till man glanced up and watched him out of the door, "There's some odd characters around" he said. "Did he just walk out without paying?" I asked. "No", said the till man, "I think he just saw those girls and followed them in for a closer look". "No way!" I said, incredulously. The till man laughed and said, a bit louder than he'd intended, "I know! There's some fucking sad bastards around here in't there!" and he slapped his palm across his mouth, looking sideways to check there were no other customers within earshot.

Things People Have Said By Way Of A Greeting Today: A woman in the middle of washing her hair: "Oh dear."; A man wearing ear defenders and three days of stubble: "Alright?"; A man wearing a football kit to lay a patio: "Hello."; A thin man with unruly grey hair, an unkempt full beard and very clean new trainers: "Ayups!"; A man in a North Face fleece: "Oh, hiya there!"; A man wearing yellow gloves to push a wheelbarrow: "Morning!"; A slim, grey-haired woman restraining a black Labrador: "Hellooo! He's a big softy."; A man of a similar age to me wearing a hooded top and tartan shorts: "Hi lad."; A very pale old man in a grey sweatshirt: "I have a lot of things wrong with me, but I'm not deaf." (After I'd knocked loudly at his door.); A man in a ski jacket and hat said nothing but raised his eyebrows and smiled; The bald man in the Fair Isle sweater said nothing and made no discernible acknowledgement of my presence, even when I said hello to him and handed him his mail. In the road outside his house, there was a dead sparrow, only about ten yards from where I saw the dead fox in March.

Wednesday, 3 October

On the post box outside the pub where Eeezi Goin' are playing on Thursday night, somebody has written 'HYC' in marker pen. I didn't know the HYC were still around; they once gave me a beating in the toilets of 'The Most Luxurious Club In The North.' I came out with two black eyes and a bust lip. It was 1988.

The proprietress of the shop is shouting into the phone in Urdu. Outside, a dope smoking, shaven-headed man shows off his new baby to his dope smoking, shaven-headed friends. They are in broad agreement that she is a right cutie.

Out in the sticks, where shreds of polythene stream like bunting from barbed wire along the fireweed verges, you can see around the corners in the cracked convex mirrors. It's all lavender and hydrangea, gravel paths and improvised containers, wellington boots, wooden windows, cabling suspended via a tree to a shed whose door is propped open with a lump of cement in the shape of a bag of cement. The sign says 'Caution, Free Range Children' and the black Lab is "deaf as a post". An old man says "Thanks, Pat", and gives me the thumbs up. I kick the ball for his dog. The first frost of the year has severed the head of the stone tortoise that stands by his door.

Friday, 12 October

On the estate where pretend owls outnumber the human population by two to one, a woman tends her plastic window boxes. She wears gold-rimmed Reactolites, pink marigold gloves, flip-flops and a grey fleece jacket and trouser combination. Her patio of pink stone flags with electric cabling running through the joints, is decorated with an assortment of garden ornamentation: a gnome riding on a snail's shell, a pair of disembodied hands holding a small bird with a solar panel in its back and a lamp in its chest, a hedgehog riding a tractor. A poodle startles the sparrows from the beech hedge. it makes me jump and I nearly trip over the statue of the top half of a woman with no arms.

11.45am: A man with mashed potato and lamb mince down the front of his shirt opens his window to offer me directions but I'm not lost. Next door, a woman with a Summer Wine perm and a grey cardigan answers her door. Her mouth is full and there's quite a large piece of flaky pastry stuck to her cheek, "Hankfs Flhuff", she says, as I hand her her parcel.

At the house that always smells of dog piss and stale cigarettes, an old man opens the window to take his mail. "You're looking very smart in your uniform today, sir", he says, "Good for you, sir. Good for you".

I cross the rec', adding another trail of footprints in the dew. A woman in a pink fleece jacket throws a blue ball with an orange launcher for her Jack Russell terrier, Muff, to fetch.

"More rubbish!" says the man at number 14 when he sees me coming, "I'm gonna put a letterbox on my dustbin so you can post it straight in" "Oh, leave him alone, he gets paid for that", says his wife from her plastic patio chair. She's thumbing through a magazine and smoking a cigarette. "Aye", says the man, "and the bin men get paid to take it away; the postman giveth and the bin man taketh away". "Aye, it keeps the world going round though dun't it, love", says the woman, winking at me.

The weather turns and the short, rotund woman with the russet dyed almost grown out perm, grey roots and purple anorak is sheltering under her blown inside-out umbrella at the bus-stop. "In't it awful weather!" she shouts across the road. I agree.

Sunday, 21 October

6.30am: The woman who feeds the pigeons by the open market is loaded up with three Jack Fulton bags of birdseed. She hides in the shadow of the architrave of entrance to the lap dancing club until the man on the ride-on street sweeping machine has disappeared behind The Christian Fellowship building.

9am: In the big new houses in the village, a drunk woman sings a reper-toire of contemporary pop songs at high volume from an open first-floor window.

10.30am: A wasp stings the back of my neck on the driveway at Shangri-La.

11.30am: A window cleaner shouts down from his ladders, "Lovely morn-ing!" I agree. "What time do you finish?" "Twenty-past-one, officially. Half-two in reality", I say. "Aye, them at t' bottom do more and more so's them at t' top

can do less and less. It's always been the way, lad. Lovely morning though. Keep smiling!"

11.45am: I spend five minutes searching for my van keys before I realise they're in my hand.

Thursday, 8 November

It's windy and the sky is littered with jackdaws, swept up like a hundred bin bags. Deep inside the bus shelter, a large woman wearing a done-up-to-the-top anorak pulls a cellophane wrapped greetings card from a large pretend-leather bag. Inspecting it, she smooths the corner between her finger and thumb; "Is that bent, or is it me?" she asks.

Also waiting for the bus is a very large man in a black tracksuit top with white trim. He's standing outside the shelter, in the middle of the pavement, feet a metre apart, squared-up against the gale. He wears his hood up, a scarf across the bottom half of his face, his hands deep in his pockets and his shoulders back; rock solid in the teeth of the squall that blows his enormous grey marl sweatpants tight around him, clearly outlining his quite small cock and balls.

"Don't worry, they're worse than they seem", says the woman, failing to reassure me as she restrains her snarling dogs.

At the house with the statuette of a meerkat holding a sign that says "Welcomes" on it, the old woman behind the glass front door gets up and walks away when I ring the bell. Her neighbour, a man who is chewing gum and wearing protective goggles comes out to tell me he thinks it's a crap day and technology is brilliant.

Friday, 16 November

Outside the Post Office, a man of about twenty who is wearing a black tracksuit with white trim and a bum-fluff moustache, slams the door of his new

silver Mercedes and swaggers over with his hands in his pockets. Without averting his eyes from the pavement, he mumbles "Move your van, boss. There's markings innit. D'ya get me?"

The man in the t-shirt, shorts and espadrilles signs for his parcel. He nods at my PDA and says "Them's weird these, aren't they?"

On the notice board at the new delicatessen, there are posters advertising classes for Zumba, Yoga for Pregnancy and a Craft Workshop. At the pub a few doors down, the chalkboard outside is advertising a Smokie tribute band.

I lean on a freshly painted door frame and get some Weathershield on my sleeve, "That's all you need, in't it?" says Mrs McHenry.

Wednesday, 21 November

The illuminated bollard in the middle of Fitzwilliam Street has been run over again. And, at the junction by the gay bar, where the upside-down shopping trolley has been on the pavement all week, the traffic lights were stuck on red.

On the bus, I sat next to the old woman who was on her way to the cemetery. She was holding a single red rose. Behind us, a group school girls were discussing which they preferred, "Eating or drinking". They unanimously agreed that drinking is definitely the best.

At the house that should be number 13 but is number 11A instead, the man with the big overcoat that restricts his movement was reversing his new car into a gate post. I judged he might not be in the mood to deal with my enquiry, so I pressed the doorbell and waited as it made a protracted series of notes of seemingly random tone, length and volume. Eventually, a woman with a tea towel slung over her shoulder answered. She apologised,

"Sorry about the bell, love. I washed it last night and it's not been right since".

Sunday, 25 November

I set off against the weather. The wind is thrashing the trees and choppy little puddles are breaching their potholes.

At the school, the headmistress comes to the door to let me in. She usually buzzes me in through the intercom. "Sorry, I couldn't see who you were; Miss Brown's not here", she explains.

I walked around the miry puddles to the house down the track by the swollen stream. I had a shoe box sized parcel for the man with the impressive sideburns. He'd hung a new front door which didn't have a letterbox. I assumed he must have relocated it, so I asked him where it was. "It's in your hand", he said, "in that parcel".

I join the queue in the shop behind the skinny white man in his twenties with the snap-back and the black tracksuit top with white trim. He's talking to the man behind the till (the Asian man with the greying bob and the pencil moustache.) "Them that ring you up about PPI innit. There's nuff jobs there! You get paid by the call. You get a headset. Even if nobody answers or they hang up, it still counts. It's done by computer."

Wednesday, 5 December

When the elderly woman with the grey Summer Wine perm says she's been drinking a lot of tea recently, the younger woman in the quilted jacket tells her it doesn't matter.

At the house on the moor, the door is ajar and I can hear people talking behind it. I knock. The conversation stops for a second, then I hear a woman say, "Who's that gonna be?" "I don't know. Why don't you open it and find out?" says a man. The door opens and a young woman with a long fringe, a quarter length fur coat and skinny jeans stands in the doorway, smoking. An older man in a grey sweatshirt with some paint splashes on it stands behind her. Before I have the chance to speak, two Cairn terriers rush snapping and yelping out from between their feet and begin nipping my ankles. "They're biting him!" says the woman, surprised. "Well, stop them then!" says the man with some urgency, "Grab them!" She doesn't move, conceding only to hold her cigarette out of harm's way. I dance around a bit and eventually step backwards over the low gate to safety, kicking off the dogs from my trouser legs as I go.

At the house with the geraniums in 'I heart Playboy' pots on the window sill, a large woman in her sixties with short cropped hair and a faded jersey pulls back the curtain when I knock at the door. I hold up her parcel and mouth "Parcel" to her. She frowns and waves me away. I assume she's somehow misunderstood, so this time I mouth "Postman", and point first to the parcel and then to her. She waves me away again and shouts at me quite loudly, "GO AWAY! I DON'T WANT ANYTHING!" I persist, holding the parcel up higher and shouting, "POSTMAN!" Finally, she lets go of the curtains and comes to the door, "Sorry love," she says, "I thought you were trying to sell me stuff".

Wednesday, 12 December

"OH, IT'S YOU!", shouts the tall man in the cardigan and trouser braces. "I WAS EXPECTING A PARCEL FROM BOOTS'!" (pronounced Bootses). I'VE BEEN EXPECTING IT FOR ABOUT FIVE DAYS NOW! I DON'T KNOW WHERE THEIR WAREHOUSE IS—OUTER MONGOLIA, I RECKON! THANKS ANYWAY LAD!"

The apostrophe and capital letters in Mrs O'Neil's name were missing, which led me to mispronounce it "Mrs One-ill". She found this so amusing that she had to

put her hand on my shoulder to steady herself.

I catch the woman wearing a green dressing gown in lieu of a coat just as she's leaving the house. "Ooh, that was lucky", she says, slipping the parcel into her enormous shoulder-mounted hand-bag and lighting herself a cigarette.

At the house with the Audi A6 on the drive and Jamie's Italy in the window, the man in the golfing sweater tells me his neighbours were unlikely to be at home because "they're coppers and they'll be out nicking someone".

I've seen three different people wearing flip-flops outside in sub-zero temperatures today.

Sunday, 23 December

5.30am: I distract a rat as it speeds across Church Lane. It runs headlong into the kerb, bounces off and lands on its back. Very briefly supine, it thrashes about inexpertly, righting itself in a shower of street lit puddle water before diving for cover under the leggy buddleia on the verge.

I saw a rat yesterday too, flat on its back. Dead. All bedraggled fur and gaping incisors. It was on the pavement outside the newsagent's shop where they display their 'value' pregnancy testing kits on the counter next to the fizzy love hearts and candy foam bananas.

Friday, 25 January 2013

As he leaves the house where the pointing has been patched with expanding foam, the man in the black tracksuit top with white trim stumbles over the soiled nappies on the doorstep. He kicks at them in frustration and then sticks two fingers up at the twelve-month-old baby who is dribbling over the shoulder of the young woman with the home-dyed ponytail as she makes her way down the steps in front of him.

Out on the main road, two other young women with home-dyed ponytails have braved the sub-zero weather conditions to have a fist fight in the middle of the street. They both successfully land several punches to each other's heads while screaming abuse and tearing at one another's vest tops. Two men in bare feet and flip-flops gingerly pick their way around them, and the ice, on their way to the bus stop.

In the rec' behind the house with seven cars on the drive and nobody ever at home, another man in a black tracksuit top with white trim pulls down the tyre from the swing and throws it at his Staffordshire bull terrier.

I see the flock of waxwings in the church gardens again, the fourth day running.

Tuesday, 5 February

6am: I walk through the park in a blizzard alongside a bow-legged man in wellingtons. His head is bare and he has an unusual yellow overcoat. His name is Patrick and he's off to Tesco's. I comment on the snow and Patrick says he'll be glad when it's gone, "I bloody fell at the bins the other day, didn't I? I was taking the rubbish out one minute, and the next I was flat on my back in the bloody snow. They say there's more in the offing and all. I'm bloody sick of it". Patrick says he doesn't envy me my job in this weather. "I bet they pay you fuck all, and all", he says. "I spent twenty years working at the hospital between 1975 and 1979 but now I don't bother because it's not worth it."

The cats in Heaton Gardens make noises like stricken toddlers.

Lots of pheasants today. Most are padding aimlessly around the verges of the farm tracks, but one was prone across Mr Etchell's knee, on an old bent-wood chair in the corner of his garage, being plucked.

The woman in the red Ford Fiesta has a large antique mantel clock on her knee. She winds down her window to ask whether I have a parcel for her. When I tell her I haven't, she says that according to the website the parcel was delivered last Friday despite the fact she only ordered it yesterday. "Maybe there's a hole in the space-time continuum?" I suggest. "No, I think they must have given me the wrong tracking number", says the woman.

It's snowing heavily again and the farm-yard is littered with dead teasels and broken plastic safety barriers. The filthy dreadlocked collie strains at the chain that tethers it to its dirty white plastic igloo kennel. In the lane, a metallic blue 4x4 BMW nearly hits me outside the house where the elderly Over 60s Club volunteer sisters live—with the Support the Lifeboats and Help for Heroes stickers in the window: "She reckons we should go down and open up but they'll not venture out in this, not them that's in their eighties!"

On the bus, the man in his sixties asks the man in his twenties whether he's "Off down The Royal Oak to watch the United game". "I thought they'd turned The Oak into a mosque." "No, they knocked that idea on the head in the end." "Well, it was never right popular when they mooted it."

Thursday, 14 February

Yesterday, on the street that smells of strong weed, a man borrowed my lighter to set fire to an old piece of coir matting. A few doors down, on the step of the end house of the terrace, the white plastic cup of water with the large dead fly floating in it and red lipstick on its rim was still there. Today, the cup is still there and there's a saturated tampon next to it as well.

There are a dozen or so coots on the beck that runs through the field off Linfit Lane, near the ring of molehills that surround the discarded CD.

I walk through the university buildings behind a young woman with long dip-dyed hair and wet-look leggings. A lowered Honda Civic skids to a halt next to her and begins revving its engine loudly. A young man with a goatee beard and a beanie hat winds down the car window and holds out a lit joint towards her. He doesn't speak and his attempt to maintain a nonchalant disposition throughout the encounter is almost successful, only betrayed at the last by the merest eye-flicker of embarrassment when the girl completely ignores him. She barely even glances up as she turns and walks away down a side street. The man winds up his window again and, wheels spinning in the gutter, he speeds away.

The tall thin man I've often seen raiding the bins for food is in WHSmith's. A dewdrop falls from his nose and lands in the pages of the boxing magazine he's reading. He closes it and puts it back on the shelf.

Wednesday, 20 February

The blackbird I often see at the entrance to the park is perched on the gates for the second day running. It doesn't fly away when I pass. It watches me. I walk within a couple of feet of it today and it doesn't flinch.

The sun is out, the sky is blue. There is birdsong: sparrows, starlings, a woodpigeon. Somebody is playing a trumpet. A car pulls away from the kerb and its tyres crackle and pop on dry asphalt. A man of about fifty, wearing double denim and a black and white bandana tied around his head, is using the phone box that I've never really noticed before.

There is horse shit in the road. Further up the valley, there are boxy 1970s brick-built semis with white fascia boards that crack loudly in the sun. There are big picture windows. There are Astras, Minis, Astras, Beetles, Astras, Minis and Astras on uneven concrete and aubretia driveways. There are monolithic decap-

itated leylandii as big as houses. There
are birch and willow, catkins and moss.
There are two pieces of litter: an empty
Muller Rice pot and a novelty shaped
luminous yellow pencil eraser. There's
a Union Jack and a Get Britain Out of
the EU poster. There are silk flowers
on the window sills. There are plastic
lawns, footballs, grit bins. There are
'moneysavingexpert.com' A4 print-outs
Blu-Tacked to porch windows saying 'No
Cold Callers'. There are whistling Eddie
Stobart collectors in t-shirts smoking
Marlboro cigarettes on hard-standings.
They build kit-cars and boats and take
things to pieces. There's the smell of
machine oil. There's the smell of cooking
oil. There are chips. There are solid
homemade repairs, gates and fences,
washers and hinges, ironmongery,
fixings and grease. There are guinea pigs
in hutches and terriers on the backs of
settees. Girls play at hopscotch and boys
dress as superheroes while they mend
punctures with holes in their knees.

A man insists I watch as he opens a
parcel. Inside it, there is a small statuette
of a blackbird perched on a twig.

Sunday, 17 March

6am and light. The sky is cloudless apart
from the gas flue vapour that leaks vertically from the houses on Church Street
and the unusual zig-zag vapour trail left
by a confused pilot above them.

I bump into Patrick again. He's wearing his unusual yellow overcoat and a
knackered black baseball cap. He tells
me he's been to the 24-hour chemist to
get some medication. He says he has the
flu and feels terrible: sweaty and cold.
He says he's been coughing all night
and that he threw-up at around 3am. I
say the usual things, "There's a lot of
it about... Get yourself home to bed...
Sweat it out... You'll be right in a few
days," and then he says goodbye and
holds out his hand, I think about it for a
second and then I shake it. When I get

to work, I go straight to the toilet and wash my hands.

Later, with dry gravel crunching under my feet and the starlings gathering in the trees above me, I swallow my first fly of the season as two considerable ladies with brooches and belts and heavy foundation pass me in a fug of something heavy by Yves Saint Laurent: "I know if I get out of the hairdressers for quarter-past I'll be all right".

Sunday, 7 April

In the street that smells of meat, the man who looks like my old headmaster is inspecting a discarded cigarette packet while a younger man, who is smoking weed and wearing headphones, does hundreds of keepie-uppies in the road.

On Easter Sunday some of the tenants of the flats were kept awake until 1.30am by loud music according to the handwritten note pinned to the front door.

I see Jonny, he's petting the beautiful Burmese cat in Warneford Road. He says he thinks it's so fine looking it could probably win Crufts even though it isn't a dog.

The gardens on the evens side of the estate are still under deep snow. At number 36, only the top of the wheelie bin with the sticker of the tropical beach scene on it is visible because of the drifting. Outside number 12, an uncomfortable looking grey-haired woman in an overcoat and Reactolite glasses is waiting at the bus stop with three drunks who are arguing over a bottle of White Lightning.

Further down, at the house with the threadbare Union-Jack doormat, an elderly woman with a tomato stain on her beige duffle coat asks me whether I've seen the bin men. "I'm seventy-six years old", she says, "They shouldn't do this to me. It's upsetting. I put it out and they've missed me again!" I

tell the woman I hadn't seen the bin men, just the Wheelie Wash man who comes along in their wake. I hand her her mail: promotional material from Boots about health and beauty products that can 'Supercharge Your Wellbeing.' "I'll not be needing that!" she says, "It's going straight in the bin—if it'll fit!"

On the main road, just down from the house called The Britvic at number 55, an elderly man with a pull-along shopping cart and thick plastic-rimmed glasses stops me. "He's mad, isn't he?" he says. "Who?" I ask. "That silly man from the government who says we can live on fifty-three pounds a week. I think he must be bloody mental! And that footballer. They've all gone bloody mental!"

When I get back to the office my workmates are reminiscing about a retired colleague who once reversed his van into his own car, touched up the damage with Dulux, and then drove to Blackpool to "dry it off". They ask me whether I remember him. I say I do, but our shifts hadn't overlapped. I used to cycle home in my trainers, so I'd leave my work boots at the office overnight where, unknown to me, for several years, he wore them for the duration of his night shift, replacing them before I arrived for work again the next morning.

Wednesday, 17 April

"Why would anyone want to punch a police horse?" asks the man on the bus, glancing up from his paper. I say I don't know.

In Primitive Street, a gust of wind blows an empty lager can from one kerb to the other while two drunks discuss the whereabouts of Amber. "Where is she?" asks the one in the faded blue anorak with the saggy pockets. "I don't know", says the other, "she spat in my face about two years ago".

A woman in her fifties in a t-shirt with a skull motif on it almost falls as she gets out of the back of a VW Golf before it has stopped. "Oh, yeah! Just reverse over me why don't you!" she yells at the driver before running across the road and slipping over on her greasy Yorkstone path. "Grrr! I'm having a really bad day!" she shouts as she gets back on her feet and rubs her hip. She opens her front door and an excited terrier shoots out and runs off down the street before she can stop it. "Now the dog's got out!"

Out on the new estate: fake-sandstone-beige and UPVC-white with accents of grit-bin and Cold-Caller-Control-Zone-sticker yellow. The background noise of burglar alarms, wind-chimes, squabbling blackbirds, shouting PE teachers and that weird clanging from the insides of swaying metal street lamps, is occasionally drowned out by the engine of the JCB whose driver is concentrating so hard that his tongue is poking out. The fake ornamental bay trees have blown over onto the plastic lawn where the high-pitched cat deterrent is repeatedly triggered by the swirling leaves and bobbing daffodils. There are sea urchins and highly glazed period folk on windowsills and solar panels on roofs. And there are dogs: people without shoes open doors while holding dogs by the collar. There are unencumbered and determined grey-haired men in navy blue fleeces pounding the streets. Teeth gritted, they march up hills, arms outstretched for extra balance along uneven nascent desire lines—past the stalled mums with their hoods up against the drizzle, pushchairs and retrievers in one hand, they reach out for their straggling toddlers with the other.

I've seen waxwings and swallows within a week of each other.

Saturday, 27 April

Another bright, sunny morning. I follow the chubby bald fifty-year-old

paperboy into the newsagent's where the man with the intense stare tries to sell me some honey roasted peanuts. "You wanna try them", he says without blinking, "They're proper nice, they are". I refuse and, as I step back outside it starts to rain heavily. The sky clouds over and the temperature drops. I think about going back and buying the nuts but the rain stops as suddenly as it had started. it stays cold though and it's a full half hour before the Reactolite lenses of the people in fleece jackets go dark again.

Outside the church hall where I was once accused of smoking 'wacky baccy' at a wedding reception, the snow that had lined the kerb has given way to dried horse shit, tree litter and slug trails. Large men walk small dogs and large women talk at the bus stop: "I was supposed to be going to Diane's but I can't walk nowhere, I'm in agony". One man's heels are overhanging the back of his Crocs by about an inch and a half. Another man, who is having his lunch at 11.30am, remarks, "Fucking hell, them Chinese give 'emselves some right names, don't they?"

I walk up the ring road behind two young men in washed out tracksuits. The taller one is walking a Staffordshire bull terrier on a lead. His swagger is so pronounced that he eventually builds up too much sideways momentum and stumbles, almost tripping over. To cover his embarrassment, he begins a vigorous air punching workout which results in his dog being yanked violently sideways with every right jab. The other man isn't paying attention to his companion, he has half his arm down the back of his tracksuit pants and is scratching his arse while he wolf whistles at the girl in dark glasses walking down the other side of the road.

Monday, 27 May

The noisy fracas among the sparrows in the hedgerow had been going on for

some time. At one point it had been so heated that it had set the dog barking. In the end, it came to an abrupt halt when the woman in the niqab shuffled past, weighed down with carrier bags full of yoghurt.

Around the corner, a woman in her fifties with a bleached blonde perm and a pink towelling bathrobe is bagging up dog shit in the middle of the road. The woman at the bus stop looks on; perhaps caught out by the warm weather, she's sweating in her heavy quilted purple anorak with a fur collar.

I was contemplating Mrs Begum's new lampshade—I'm pretty sure it's upside-down—when my attention was drawn to a passing young woman whose facial complexion didn't match that of her décolletage by some distance. It was, however a near perfect match for her flesh coloured leggings.

The thin woman in the skinny jeans is making a noisy phone call while supervising two toddlers in the park. "If they're trying to take the piss again, they can kiss my arse!" she says, before breaking off suddenly to reprimand the children. Muting the phone with her hand, she shouts, "Hit her back! Fucking hit her back! Fucking hell, Jade, stop being such a fucking wuss!"

As the morning wears on, the streets fill up with massive men in enormous shirts eating pasties from paper bags. They mainly call each other "Pal" and discuss cars. "You didn't pay much for the Punto, did you?" "Five-and-a-half. Mind you, I only got five for the Audi."

Wednesday, 19 June

Strong shadows. Stained asphalt: oil, moss, blackened chewing gum, blobs of melted chocolate, strange bleached footprints, a criss-cross of tyre tracks in a patch of spilt concrete, lichen (Is it lichen or is it bird shit?) broken glass that glistens in the gutter, dust (not mud), the

long dribble of white paint from the top of Orchard Terrace down to where that man is always mending his Volvo. The man who is always mending his Volvo has a sweat on today; he has ordered the wrong size cylinder-head O-rings.

Two filthy men in a knackered transit pickup with old household radiator greedy-boards crawl by, eyeing the gardens for junk. The passenger, a skinny man with a torn t-shirt and a missing tooth, holds up a pornographic centrefold out of the window as they pass, "My bird!" he yells to me. "Super", I say. "My bird!" he yells again, even louder.

There's a swarm of long-tailed tits in the park and, later out in the sticks, I hear a cuckoo.

At the building site, I am referred to as 'Pal', 'Bud', 'Mate', and 'Fella' during the course of a single thirty-second encounter with a man with pumped-up arms, a high-vis vest and a t-shirt with '5UCK MY D1CK' written on it in a distressed sans serif with a drop shadow.

Down by the big new church that looks like a multi-storey car park, someone has discarded a pair of brand new trainers. They're positioned in the middle of the pavement, a foot apart and slightly splayed at the toes, as if somebody caught up in the rapture hadn't fastened their laces properly.

The missing cat posters that have been on the lamp-posts for months have suddenly bleached blue in the last week.

Saturday, 6 July

The short but substantial man with the unruly hair, sun visor, t-shirt, steel toe-capped boots and cargo shorts with a large bunch of keys attached to the belt says, "Hello, Kevin" as I pass. He's propping an old glass panelled front door up against the cellar doorway of the working men's club. I have no idea how he knows my name.

On the edge of the moor, at the end terrace with the imitation stone grotesques on the garden wall, the imitation leaded lights in the windows and the imitation wooden front door, Mrs Dyson's bathrobe has blown from the rotary washing line, over the garden wall and onto the windscreen of the red Ferrari 348 that is parked in the road.

Around the corner, an indiscrete drug deal is taking place; a young man wearing a snapback baseball cap has double-parked his hatchback next to another young man wearing a snapback baseball cap in a different hatchback. They begin exchanging small packages through adjacent windows. After a couple of minutes, the double parked young-man-in-a-baseball-cap pulls over to the kerb, gets out of his hatchback and gets into the other man's passenger seat where the two of them smoke a very strong smelling joint together.

Saturday, 20 July

The small grey pony is pulling the large brown pony's mane and tail. Every so often, the brown one retaliates but it only puts the grey off for a few seconds before it starts again. They've been at it for at least twenty minutes.

Earlier, after I'd set off a chain of barking dogs by walking through the estate, I passed the big woman in the sunglasses, vest top and tattoos. She was parked-up in a silver Astra making a loud phone call: "Gary only came out for a smidgeon, then he's gone back inside the house!"

A man and his grandson are having a tetchy argument as they buff opposite alloys of a five-year-old Ford Fiesta. "Why do you keep saying that when you know it's not true?" repeated the grandson for the third time.

In the sticks, old men in flat caps and short-sleeved khaki shirts drive immaculate ten-year-old saloons around the lanes, their wing mirrors thrashing through overgrown leylandii, dead flies accumulating on the plastic remembrance day poppies cable-tied to their radiator grills. There is honeysuckle everywhere.

It's hot. The road is sticky and the weeds on the verges have turned to straw. Shiny men wearing nothing but shorts and trainers make busy noises. Past the derelict asylum and the road cone with the Greggs bag stuffed into the top, I knock my hat off on a washing line next to the parked milliner's van. The man at the bus stop whose trousers are riding so low that his pubeless cock cleavage is clearly visible, laughs out loud.

Sunday, 4 August

In my haste to catch the bus, I almost collide with the fully loaded, seven foot high floral display unit on wheels. A thin man in a tracksuit is pushing it down the street to the entrance of The Bargain Shop. He parks it up and attaches an A4 handwritten sign to it with sellotape: 'MEGA CHEAP CHEESE IN FRIDGE'.

I miss my bus. I watch it go by as I'm telling the tall man in the mauve shirt and black, pleat-front straight-cut short-leg perma-crease trousers how to get to the Ann Summers shop.

Chapel Street smells of perming solution again. Struggling up it, the old woman with swollen ankles and two bags of shopping says, "I wish someone would turn this bloody hill round".

I compliment the elderly man on his work: he's been building a shed all week and it is impressively level, despite the extreme incline of the ground it's built on. I shout over to him three or four times but I think he must be hard of hearing because he just smiles and makes comments about the weather and an appointment at the hospital he's got to remember.

On the estate where elderly women with perms, mid-calf length skirts and sandals walk terriers and knock on one another's doors holding polythene bags, I've been stopping for a chat with the man with the southern accent who sits outside his house on a mobility scooter. Today, he's not there. His wife is though, on an old bentwood chair on the patio next to the statue of a meerkat with a magpie's feather glued into its paw. "Your mate's not here today," she says to me "He's gone down there to get some rolls", she waves an arm in the direction of the shops, "He calls teacakes 'rolls'!" she laughs.

Sunday, 1 September

At the bus stop, the man with the grey beard, striped polo-shirt and large silver watch is bent over scratching both his knee and his elbow at the same time. Across the road, another man with a striped shirt and grey beard is painting his gate bright yellow for the second day running. Further up the road, at the next bus stop, a young man in a baseball cap and headphones is dancing enthusiastically by himself. And, around the corner, on Cross Lane, I see the same man delivering the same flyers to the same houses he was yesterday.

Six squirrel sightings today: two in trees, one running along the edge of a skip and three dead in the road.

Somebody has lit a bonfire too close to the Costcutter. Even inside the shop, the smoke is acrid. A teenage couple stand outside: he has a tattoo on his neck and is gobbing on the floor, she is wafting the smoke from her face with her cigarette hand and hoicking her grey marl sweatpants out of her arse crack with the other.

A Ford Fiesta goes past in too low a gear.

On the estate with the diverse and imaginatively improvised garden furniture, a boy on a BMX stops me as I am unloading my van: "Are you Postman Pat?" "No. Postman Pat's got a helicopter now. I've only got this rusty old van." "Postman Pat is ugly anyway" says the boy "He hasn't got a helicopter. He hasn't even got a black and white cat. He hasn't got owt. He's ugly and he goes on eBay!"

At the gap in the wall where the stone was stolen, the thin lorry driver with the blue overalls and round glasses is drinking tea from a Thermos mug. "There won't be any stone left in Huddersfield at this rate!" he says.

Somebody has stolen the top-stones from Mrs Taylor's garden wall and last night somebody unscrewed the hinges of my shed door.

Saturday, 21 September

Down from where the giant mechanical dinosaur has been tearing at the walls of the old YMCA building, three short men were pulling on green hi-vis jackets and switching on an improvised lightbox sign: 'Hand Car Wash Now Open'. 300 yards further down the road again, a short man in a grey tracksuit was dwarfed by the seven foot high sandwich board that he was dragging out onto the pavement: 'Hand Car Wash Now Open'.

The weather has turned. In the sticks, people in trademarked waterproof fabrics suffixed with 'tec', swarm around the blackberry bushes in the lanes while streams of run-off carry acorns, twigs and beechnut husks around their Brashers.

In town, flies bask in the last of the residual heat from the white UPVC doors and fascia boards. I disturb some of them when I knock at a house on Moss Street and get a face full. They're swarming around the overflowing green re-cyclers that the new students have mistaken for normal refuse bins too. The bin men have refused to take them and left them on the pavements along the length of Elm Street.

The golf club is swarming with regional representatives of the Kitchen and Bathroom industry at their annual networking event. A man with a receding hairline, grey slacks and a fleece jacket steps out of a van decorated with a wraparound livery featuring a naked young woman enjoying a shower. "Have you ever watched that *Doc Martin*?" the man asks his companion. "With Martin Clunes?" his companion responds "Yes, that's the one, it's fucking shit hot".

On my way home, a woman on a mobility scooter begins shouting abuse and gesticulating wildly towards me as I approach. I cross the road towards her and, as I get nearer she shouts "It's all right love, I'm talking to myself!"

Sunday, 29 September

I give Molly a lift home from school. "This week has gone so quickly", she says, "I can't believe it's nearly next weekend already". We pass the bus stop where a man dressed as a ninja with two sticks of french bread under his arm is struggling to light a cigarette without dropping them.

It's bright and sunny again. Out in the sticks, I can hear power tools and dogs barking half a mile away. A couple in their sixties wearing matching plaid shirts (hers accessorised with a brown leather belt at the waist) are walking perfectly in step through the village. They synchronously tear pieces from their pasties and chew in unison. When somebody they know passes them in a car, they notice simultaneously, both glancing up at the same time before breaking into smiles and holding aloft their right hands to wave.

An old woman is talking to her gardener about the neighbour who has recently returned from a holiday abroad: "Have you seen his suntan?

He's so dark! I didn't want to let him in. I don't usually let people that colour in the house!"

Autumn spiders have moved in on the flies that have been basking on the white UPVC doors. Silk shrouded baubles of pre-digested carcass dangle from the pretend wooden beading, bobbing silently in the light breeze.

Friday, 11 October

It's been windy today and the bird shit stained section of the road below the canopy of the trees at the entrance to the estate is now completely covered with leaves.

A woman with Cosmic Purple hair and a boat neck Breton shirt walks a black cat on a lead around the perimeter of her garden. She stretches out her left hand for support against the gable wall as she negotiates the narrow gravel path which is lined on both sides with a variety of cat statuettes.

An elderly woman with a nicotine yellow perm and a purple anorak passes me. She's conducting a loud conversation with a man in a beanie hat and an enormous jumper: "Well, he's pissing in the bed", says the man. "Well, that's not good", says the woman. "Well, he can't get out, can he?" "Well, can't they give him a bedpan?" "Well, he can't feel his legs, can he?" "Well, he needs a catheter, doesn't he? Will they not give him a catheter?" "Well, they won't. They say he can get out of bed but he just doesn't want to."

There are yard brushes leant against unnecessary porches and charity bags containing mainly jigsaws on the driveways. Starlings attempt a small murmuration and harassed lapwings stalk worms in the back field. A woman in a rusty coloured fleece jacket shows me the cut on her thumb. "I've knackered my hand unblocking the drain", she says, "That's what happens when you don't have a man about".

Saturday, 9 November

I knock at a door on the estate of Range Rovers and shop-bought topiary where the fake cobblestones still have their barcode stickers on them. Inside the house, a dog barks enthusiastically while a woman implores it to "Stay in there, you!" Eventually, the door shudders open to reveal the woman in a Fair Isle onesie, holding the dog by its collar. "He's just bloody humped the gas man", she explains, "I'm not letting him near you!"

It's quiet around here among the lawns, the winter flowering pansies, the lavender, and the leylandii. There are more tradesmen's vans than residents' cars during the day. Occasionally, a disembodied arm extends from an open window to shake crumbs from a tea towel, or an immaculate twelve-year-old Nissan Primera reverses slowly from a driveway. On the pavement outside the pebble-dashed inter-war bungalow with the rotten timber frames and the dangerous chimneys, a cat is fighting with a marigold glove. Further down, where the three empty cider bottles have been left in a neat row under the hawthorn, an elderly man hobbles by in a threadbare camel-hair coat secured at the waist with packing tape. In the gutter, a light breeze fans the pages of a discarded Max Hastings book and, at the bottom of the cul-de-sac, an old woman bends to pick up a Virgin Media flyer from her door-mat, "Red hot sale!" she says, rolling her eyes, "That's going straight in the bin! I don't even believe in Richard Branson!"

Monday, 25 November

At the entrance to the park, a shaggy Border collie called Chicken is being restrained by its owner: "No, Chicken! Leave it! Chicken! No!"

Around the corner at the house with the new pattern imprinted concrete driveway, I eventually realise that the large polished red and white streaked calcite sphere on the window sill isn't the back of the head of an elderly man with a ruddy complexion and a wispy white comb-over, and I stop trying to attract its attention.

Back in town, an enormous man driving a Mini passes me as I walk under the stalactites that hang from the arch of the railway bridge. He clatters noisily over the steel road plates that cover the pothole at the entrance to Tesco's car park, parks across two spaces and hoists himself out by grabbing the door frame with both hands.

The golf pro' with the Hoxton fin hairstyle cranes his neck to watch the small yellow aeroplane from the nearby airfield as it flies low overhead.

At one of the houses that backs onto the green, a thin bald man in a fleece jacket and faded jeans is carefully stencilling the names 'Brian' and 'Susan' onto the backrest of a wooden bench in a swirly gold font. I pass him as he's admiring his work. He glances up and waves briefly before walking up the gravel path, past the little tableau on the lawn: a stone tortoise apparently engaged in combat with a tiny plastic second world war infantryman that has been painted white. At the entrance to the conservatory, the man places his unlit roll-up on the window sill, kicks off his boots and disappears inside behind a bookcase of faded hardback autobiography spines: Botham, Clough, Greavsie…

Saturday, 21 December

The old man with the bag-for-life and the beige anorak at the bus stop hasn't got a Mohican hairstyle, it's a shadow cast by a lamppost across his bald head by the low winter sun.

The sky blows from black to blue and back again: leaves, jackdaws, Tesco bags, starlings and fieldfares windswept under brief rainbows.

All morning, the police helicopter has been hovering above the estate where armed police are shouting at a man in a t-shirt decorated with distressed appliqué text.

At the other end of the road, the young woman with the big afro is reading a psychology textbook while two fat men in black satin shirts, elaborate tattoos, shiny grey slacks and light tan, chisel-toe mock-crocodile shoes carry large boxes into her house and call her darling.

A few doors up, a man with a strong eastern European accent explains from an upstairs window why he can't open his front door, "I bought a couch. It is too big. I can't open the door".

The contents of the next house down have been dumped in miry puddles in the front garden: a pair of Ugg boots, a hi-fi system, a two-foot-tall vase, an upside-down sofa…

I park up next to a discarded boat and drink coffee from a flask while a man smoking weed with his coat only half on, takes his small daughter to the newsagent in her reindeer onesie.

Sunday, 19 January 2014

A grey Vauxhall Zafira pulls up on the canal bank next to the narrowboat with the big spotlights—just down from where they pulled the dead paedophile out of the water in the Christmas holidays. A man gets out and sweeps half a dozen McDonalds take-out cups from the footwell and onto the towpath. He brushes crumbs from his fleece jacket and boot-cut jeans, stretches, gets back into the car and drives away.

The shadows of the people in the bus queue are long. The man I used to think looked too young to smoke a pipe is there, smoking a pipe. He doesn't look too young anymore. On the wall beside the shelter, someone has written 'I know' with a marker pen.

Hundreds of geese fly over in a noisy quarter-mile 'V' formation. The white

UPVC front door of the house opposite opens—the one with the fake leaded lights in the shape of a Yorkshire rose—and Mr Mohammed steps outside in salwar kameez and sandals. He stands next to the soggy carpet in his front yard and looks up at the birds, shielding his eyes from the sun. Next door, the man in the torn gilet and jeans has also heard the noise and comes outside. He leans on his door frame holding a mug of tea in one hand, shielding his eyes with the other, his digestive biscuit held between his teeth. The two men stare up at the birds until they've all passed, briefly acknowledge one another and then go back inside, closing their front doors in unison.

Saturday, 1 February

As I pass the single, left-footed bowling shoe in the gutter—just before the pub chalkboard that's had 'Bitchcraft' written on it for weeks—a young man in a black tracksuit with white trim passes loudly, standing up on an exhausted old scooter. "That'll be stolen", says the toothless man with the tattoo teardrop from under his threadbare hoodie, "It's a wonder he's got a helmet on".

Mr Mahmood has paved over the paving that he paved over his garden with. He's laid some new, bright yellow concrete flags over the old cracked ones. He has used no bedding, mortar or fixture of any kind except at the edges where the flags adjoin his crumbling garden wall; just a lumpy smeared trail of cement runs around the perimeter joints.

Out in the sticks now, the wind is thrashing the trees and the sleet is thrashing my face as I slide around on slimy untreated millstone. It's been wet and windy for weeks. The verges are scarred with deep miry tyre tracks and streams of run-off carry tree litter and even small branches along in the gutter. They are blasting at the quarry

and a massive swirling flock of gulls is screeching overhead.

Two bald men in black tracksuits with white trim are overseeing the cross country run around the perimeter of the school grounds. Dozens of teenagers straggle through the gap in the wall and splash past, all muddy ankles and too big t-shirts. A small, skinny boy with thick blond hair tells the taller heavier boy alongside him, "I was the fittest person with an inhaler at my old school".

In the valley bottom, where the moss on the dry stone walls is almost fluorescent, I watch a pair of herons flap by and disappear over the horizon where you can see the tips of the wind turbines on the moor.

At the cottage with the electric gates, a delivery driver rolls his eyes and says, "Twat", not quite under his breath as he tries to write out a form in a squall.

Tuesday, 18 February

The woman with the bit of cake on her face looks perplexed at the pair of boxing gloves in the road. It's raining hard, occasionally sleeting, and the deluged streets dance in reflected light.

I cross to the street that's lined with empty pizza boxes, food tins, cooking sauce jars, energy drink cans, navy blue underpants, cerise pink shoes with missing heels, rolls of sodden carpet, mattresses, children's plastic ride-on toys, a sofa, broken glass, an empty satnav box, and a massive burst-open bag of aggregate. Near the top, at one of the houses where they have sold all the stone flags from the yard and replaced them with dog shit, the woman with the tattoos and the bathrobe says, "Ooo, it's snowing!" "I know", I say. "I take it you don't like snow." "No, not really, it's a bit inconvenient." "Haha! I do", she says, as she closes the door and disappears back inside her warm dry house.

Next door, the stocky terrier on the windowsill is on its hind legs, pulling down the curtains, its cock flopping from side to side as it scrabbles its front paws against the glass, trying to get a better purchase.

It's still raining when I knock at the house with the crumbling concrete driveway to tell the owner that the driver's door of the S-Class Mercedes saloon with the low profile tyres, is wide open. A man in his late-twenties answers. He wears a meticulously manicured beard, three-quarter length tracksuit pants, flip-flops and a t-shirt. "Yeah", he laughs, "I got to take it to the scrappers. Cheers, mate".

Sunday, 9 March

Two thin young men in baseball caps and bum fluff are eating eggs in the café on Westbourne Road, a copy of *The Sun* open on the table in front of them. "He paid £106,000 to look like that!" says

the one in the white hat, poking his yolky knife at a picture of a semi-naked man with very pronounced abdominal muscles. "Why?" says the man in the blue hat. "Because he's a fucking knob."

At the Costcutter on the other side of the road, a young woman in a polka-dot onesie, heavy make-up, drawn on eyebrows and a big 'up do' is waiting outside in the drizzle with two Staffordshire bull terriers. A large truck passes, blowing over the steel *Huddersfield Examiner* sandwich board with a crash and the dogs yelp in surprise.

Later, out in the sticks, a pair of frogs are in amplexus on the steps of the house that once featured on TV's *Grand Designs* and a sparrowhawk kills a wood pigeon on Mr and Mrs Mitchell's driveway. As I cross the road by the Conservative Club, my hat blows off and a woman under an umbrella walks into me as I bend down to retrieve it.

On the estate, the man who always wears the same baggy tracksuit bottoms and unusual cap-sleeved t-shirt says he's looking forward to some nicer weather because it puts people in a better mood. Further down, in the car park by the flats, the old man in the tweed suit shouts "We're getting posh, aren't we?" to the Rastafarian man who is fitting some new wheel trims to his Vauxhall Astra.

Back in town, the drunk man in the grey suit is emptying his catheter bag into the storm drain by the bedroom furniture shop.

Tuesday, 1 April

The wind picks up and Mrs O'Leary's wind chimes chime while the scrap men throw the TV over the broken fence. Further down, the jolly old overweight racist man with the moustache and the 1970s zip-up raglan cardigan with suedette detail is hiding the Asian children's toys behind the wall at the bus stop again. Down by the house with the ceramic cart horse in the porch, the kestrel perched on the steering wheel of the builder's van stares as I pass. Next door, the woman who always calls me "My dear" is wearing her red coat with the leopard fur trim. She unloads Lidl and Wilko bags from a taxi, pays the driver and carries all six bags up her path at once, past the countless woodland creature garden ornaments that incorporate solar panels and lamps. I wave and she shouts "Hello, my dear!"

A funeral cortège led by a man in a top hat and a cane passes through the estate. Mrs Perkins adjusts her vest top and puts out her cigarette, "I don't know who that was", she says, "but you should always pay your respects, shouldn't you?"

At the large, detached houses near the park, an elderly man in a fleece jacket tells me, "Steam railways make life worth living".

At the house next-door-but-three—with the black BMW on the drive—another elderly man in a fleece jacket is in the garage. He's working at a Black & Decker Workmate while he listens to Ken Bruce play The Three Degrees on Radio 2. A Tesco delivery van arrives. The driver is also listening to Ken Bruce playing The Three Degrees on Radio 2, "How are you?" he shouts to the Black & Decker man. "I'd be a lot better if the sun was shining!" the Black & Decker man replies.

At the golf club, the four grey haired golfers in black fleece jackets have gathered around the bearded, grey haired golfer in the black fleece jacket to ask him how much they owe him. It transpires that three of them owe him £25 and one of them owes him £28.

Tuesday, 29 April

"I was out in fucking Leeds at the weekend", says the man sitting in front of me on the bus. "There's some fucking talent over there compared to Huddersfield, you know? It's a different world." "You need some bromide", says the man with the bent glasses next to him. "Bromide? What's bromide?" "It'll calm you down, stop you thinking about it all the time." "But I like thinking about it!" I look out of the window; a plump woman with thick dry curly hair is sitting at the lights in her mauve Vauxhall Corsa eating yoghurt from the pot with a metal spoon.

At the house with the single gatepost and a gate but no fence or wall etc., nothing to mark its boundary with the pavement, a boy of about ten years is standing and staring, his face smeared with streaks of fake tan. "How come you're just standing there?" he asks the delivery man, who's writing out a card on the step of the house next door. "How come you're just standing there?" the delivery man asks back. "I don't know", says the boy.

Out in the sticks, surrounded by dog groomers' vans, the sun comes out and flies bounce off my face. Trees cast dappled shadows across ivy-covered walls that buzz with insects. I hear a cuckoo, see dunlins, lapwings, pheasants, (close-up) swallows, ducks, geese, and a beautiful peacock butterfly, all within half an hour. Back in town, Craig Bainbridge tells me he's seen two ducks eating some chips outside C. Booth's hardware shop. He says he'd have taken a photo but he was on his scooter.

Results of an hour spent researching what to wear in the countryside at this time of year: knitted beige lurex cardigan—no sleeves, tied at waist; brown hoodie; green overalls; green anorak with hood—North Face; black and navy woollen jumper; hi-vis coat—green/muddy; pink polo-neck jumper with black gilet; navy blue overall/shop coat; fleece jackets—various and sundry; blue cagoule—torn; green zip-up raglan cardigan; light blue cotton shirt; t-shirts—various and sundry.

Thursday, 29 May

Four women in their thirties pass me near the junction box that has been vandalised with the slogan 'WALTER SCOTT IS A BATTY BOY'. They walk two abreast, arms folded tight, the hoods of their bathrobes pulled over their heads against the driving rain. The old man whose garden smells of chives is putting out his bins. He watches the women pass and rolls his eyes, blood from a nosebleed congealing thickly on his top lip.

Out in the sticks: the sun comes out and there are dog walkers with ski poles, gaiters and fleece jackets. Only the pony's head is visible above the sea of yellow in the buttercup field. There are rhododendrons, striped lawns, BMWs, Range Rovers, and those panelled front doors that look like enormous choco-late bars. Queues of men in shorts and t-shirts stand outside the Sandwich Barn—pumped up torsos and skinny legs—and the old man in full motorcycle racing leathers pulls off his helmet to reveal a somehow immaculate and astonishing 1970s hairdo.

Right out in the sticks: the sun is out but the cow-parsley lined roads are still littered with leaves and twigs after all the wind and rain. Crows scatter as I approach. There are broken Zafiras, Vitaras, ancient Land Rovers, and mucky trainers. There are midges too, and I think I saw a lone oystercatcher down by the reservoir. Puffs of pollen explode from the pine trees and I definitely heard a cuckoo.

Friday, 6 June

"You know her from number 14?" says Mrs Kaur in the shop, "Well, every time she comes in here she's different: one day she's a goth, one day she's like, normal, like, white, normal, and then yesterday she came in and she was a bloody Muslim!"

On Union Street, Mr Coldwell is in his yard trying to spray an old push-bike yellow in the rain. He says it's for the window display of the florist's shop on the route of the Tour de France. He's well into his second can of paint but the rain is washing it off as fast as he can spray it on. "I should have waited for a finer day, it looks crap", he explains. At the house next door, they have finished laying their new plastic lawn and have now embellished it: in one corner stands a plastic statuette of mole wearing a miner's helmet and, in another, a shiny fake plastic dog turd.

On the new estate, a magpie is squawking hysterically and dive-bombing the fat black cat which eventually hides underneath a Suzuki Vitara for cover. A bit further down, the young mum is struggling to load baby equipment around the large custom built speaker

system in the boot of the new VW Polo. A bit further down again, next to the children's playground that the children never play on, a man with a good two-thirds of his arse showing is mending his old Transit Connect. "Can I borrow your drill, Trevor?" he shouts to the man drinking beer in his front garden, "You cheeky bastard!" the man shouts back.

Sunday, 22 June

Just down from the Sun pub where 'Elvis' performed last night, the man who still has his Christmas decorations up is singing Everly Brothers songs at the top of his voice while he does his ironing with the window open.

Two fifteen-year-old Vauxhall coupés driven by young snapback wearers speed past. The silver metallic one in front hits the speed-bump by the bus stop too quickly and its wide-arch body kit comes off in one piece. The follow-ing coupé, a red one, hits the body kit and drags it up the road for about fifty yards, smashing it to pieces. The elderly man with the Scottish accent and the spaniel asleep in the basket attached to his walking-frame says, "There're some right fucking idiots about, aren't there?"

On the terrace of houses with more plants in the guttering than in the gardens, a man of about sixty, wear-ing a sweatshirt, jeans, and slippers sits on his front step listening to The Eurythmics at very high volume. He occasionally joins in with the chorus between drags on his roll-up.

Out in the sticks, builders of all ages listen to eighties chart hits all day long and chubby young white men with no socks, beards, tattoos and flat caps say, "Thanks, boss", to the Asian shopkeeper or do some cycling. In front of the market cross, the man of about sixty with the grey crew-cut and rat-tail

discusses his Mercedes with another younger Mercedes owner. They both refer to their cars using the pronouns 'she' and 'her'.

Saturday, 19 July

Under the overgrown brambles, through the spiders' webs, past the tethered cat asleep on the lawn at the limit of its chain, to Mr Briggs' front door. "Good weekend?" he asks. "Not so bad, thanks. You?" "It were all right. We went down The Railway. I said to Robert, 'Have you any food on?' He said 'Yes, we're doing bacon sandwiches for a pound.' I said, 'I'll have two.' So we had a bacon sandwich each." "Very nice", I say. "Aye, but when I got up to go for a piss, they had a bloke on the toilet door trying to charge me 50p because of the Tour de France! The robbing bastards! I said to Robert, 'You're not charging me 50p for a piss, I've been coming in here thirty-five year.'" "Did he charge you?" I said. "Did he fuck. Robbing bastard!"

The roofers are listening to Tracey Chapman on their bright yellow, heavy-duty site radio while they discuss their nights out in Brighouse. "Aye, I went out there last weekend. It wasn't a bad night but I didn't go out to get rat-arsed," says the younger one, rolling a cigarette. "Fuck me!" says the older one, "I did! I got absolutely fucking bladdered."

The occupants of the little Fiat 500 ahead of me at the lights are engaged in some kind of gobbing-out-of-the-window contest. The big man with the moustache in the near-side passenger seat appears to be winning; he's landed a large greeny halfway across the pavement outside the doctor's surgery. Two of the beige pensioners in the long line of mainly-beige-with-accents-of-navy pensioners at the bus stop look on disapprovingly. They begin to remonstrate with the Fiat men but the wind blows something heavy by Yves St Laurent into my van so I wind up my window and miss what they say.

Tuesday, 19 August

I chase the cloud shadows up over the moor and onto the estate where the men still drive Rovers and wear their hair in elaborate combovers that flip up in the wind like busy, beige peddle-bin lids. Wind-assisted lapwings flock in the field behind the abandoned Renault camper, the pretend duck by the bin store 'quacks' as I pass, and a replica of a basset hound peers out from the large stone handbag in Mrs Hinchliffe's Alpine rockery, its head bobbing on a spring. People in comfy shoes restrain small terriers, fry liver and onions, smoke cigarettes, and scrape fluvial sediment from a storm drain with a butter knife. A man with a bit of dinner on his face sits on a collapsible chair outside his conservatory door. He is surrounded by marigolds, begonias, gladioli, Sport For All stickers, a faded Basil Ede print of some ducks, a pile of VHS video cassettes, a dozen or so pretend meerkats, and a miniature wooden wheelbarrow stuffed with pansies and snapdragons. Next door, a ten-year-old dusty-pink Kia Picanto pulls up and a grey-haired man with thick, plastic-rimmed Reactolite glasses and a three-quarter length beige anorak climbs out. He slams the door, opens the boot, and unloads three heavy looking Lidl bags-for-life. He pulls out a small packet of dog biscuits and holds it up high to show the man with the dinner on his face who shouts, "Thanks, Derek!" and points towards the open door of his green plastic shed, "Wob us it in there, can you?"

Sunday, 24 August

"Kyle's always grabbing my tits", says the young woman in the tight fitting playsuit whose toddler son has just grabbed her tits. "I know! Mine too, it really hurts", says the older woman in the noteworthy trainers as she gathers her low-maintenance hair into a scrunchie. "And it's embarrassing", adds the younger one, as she pushes her unfashionable specs up the bridge of her nose.

The butcher is recommending a cut of pork loin to the thin-lipped elderly woman with the big black canvas shopping bag and frown. He waves a large knife over it in the display counter, "That'll be lovely; tender as a woman's heart!" he says. "I'll have the sausages", says the woman.

A boy of about six or seven years old stops me in the street. "Do you want to buy this for a pound?" he says, opening his palm to reveal the pebble I've just seen him pick up from Mr Beever's driveway. "What is it?" I ask. "A pebble", says the boy, rubbing it on his sleeve, "It's shiny". "A pound for a pebble?" I say. "It's magic", says the boy.

I was watching a nuthatch in Hangingstone Road when a thin man in washed-out black passed at dangerously high speed. He was riding a pushbike and trailer with GAY written across the back of it in large plastic letters. He looked up at me as he shot through the narrow gap between the double parked cars. "Hiya!" he yelled at the top of his voice. The nuthatch flew away.

Tuesday, 9 September

Out in the sticks where fifty percent of women are inside a Range Rover, I follow the deer down the gravel driveway to the barn conversion where the new faux-modernist chrome plated garden sculpture is "something a bit different" and "absolutely beautiful to look at" according to the woman with the "glass of something lovely" in her hand. I lost a fiver around here yesterday, I retrace my steps for about ten minutes but there's no sign of it.

In the village, the grown-up paper-girl in distressed denim passes me in the street. She tucks her phone under her chin and folds a copy of *The Sun* for her next drop without pausing her conversation, "She's having another baby", she says, "Royal twats!" She pushes open the gate with her hip, "…Yes, well, if I had a decent job I wouldn't be doing a paper round, would I?"

I park my van at the end of another long driveway—in the same place I have every day this week. I open the door and there, screwed up on the pavement, is my fiver.

Sunday, 21 September

I've walked a long way today; through eight spiders' webs. I've got dead flies webbed to my shirt and face.

There's tree litter, there are bagged nappies, and there are BMWs on the slippery Driveways of Distinction.

On the main road, a builder is loading a heavy-duty site radio back into his van. He slams the doors shut as I stride across his freshly laid concrete path leaving three deep footprints. I apologise and made a weak joke about the current vogue for pattern imprinted concrete. The builder says nothing, just turns around, opens the van doors, and unloads his radio and tools again. I disappear around a corner and wash my shoes in a puddle.

A small boy of about four or five years old runs out across the road. His dad comes after him, picks him up and drags him back to the pavement. "I've told you not to do that, It's dangerous!" He yells. "I know," says the boy. "So why did you do it then?" "Because it was a secret ninja job."

Thursday, 2 October

Research into outdoor chores carried out in the last week of September: Male, 40s, watering potted annuals: t-shirt, jeans, sandals. Male, 70s, scrubbing hose reel with stiff brush: t-shirt, trousers, sandals. Male, 60s, clipping fingernails: t-shirt, jeans,

sandals. Female, 60s, digging out couch grass: fleece jacket, jogging pants, walking boots. Female, 70s, taking seedlings round to a neighbour: blouse, trousers, sandals. Female, 40s, walking Labrador: t-shirt, jeans, trainers. Female, 70s: weeding between driveway setts with special long-handled tool: fleece jacket, trousers, sandals. Male, 60s, loading garden cuttings into Fiat Punto: fleece jacket, jeans, black shoes. Female, 40s, re-pointing garage wall: fleece jacket, tracksuit pants, slippers. Female, 70s, walking Highland terrier: fleece jacket, knee-length plaid pleated skirt, flat black shoes. Male, 60s, re-pointing wall: polo-shirt, jeans, black shirt. Female, 30s, putting out bins: large knitted striped jumper, jogging pants, one slipper, one bare foot. Female, 70s, popping to shop to get bits: knee-length skirt, knitted cardigan, flat black shoes. Male, 60s, sweeping yard: fleece jacket, trousers, welly shoes. Male, 60s, washing Fiat Punto: navy-blue overalls, black shoes. Male, 60s, clearing guttering: shirt with collar, V-neck sweater, suit trousers, slippers. Female, 60s, sweeping pavement outside house: cardigan, trousers, slippers. Male, 80s, polishing Kia Picanto: shirt with collar, v-neck sweater, suit trousers, black shoes. Female, 70s, sweeping driveway with brand new yard-brush: sweatshirt embroidered with floral display, trousers, welly shoes. Male, 70s, re-applying window putty: knitted cardigan, jeans, slippers. Male, 50s, shouting abuse at a neighbour in the street, "Don't fuck with me!": t-shirt, jeans, socks. Male, 70s, telling the postman that a neighbour has died, "Yep, they've buried her and everything.": baseball cap, cardigan, jogging pants, trainers. Male, 20s, hiding door key under mat, "You never saw that, did you? There's nowt worth nicking anyway, it's a right shit-hole.": motorcycle helmet, tracksuit, trainers.

Thursday, 16 October

It's been a windy night and the beech nuts are popping under my feet. The street lights are out again and it would be pitch black were it not been for the faint glow of the light that illuminates the green lichen triangle that used to be a street sign.

Lunchtime: still only half light. And cold. Paths are lined with thick puddles of leaves, black arthritic nettles, and frantically suckering brambles. The wind hisses through yellow horse chestnut, and telegraph wires strain at their poles. Brown fields are dotted white with gulls and the farm cat swallows a mouse whole in just three gulps.

At the pub in the village where '2 Dine for £12.99 on selected main courses and afternoon tea', the landlord is being important enough in Fair Isle and corduroy. "Hello there!" he enthuses to customers disgorged crease free from mainly Range Rovers.

I watch some squabbling jackdaws while I piss against a tree. Half a dozen of them are fighting over the topmost perch of the church steeple. They circle scrappily for a while until one suddenly tips its wing and attempts a landing. Usually, its move is pre-empted by the others and the breakaway bird is knocked off course and forced to abort. Occasionally, one succeeds in making the perch only for the rest to rush it en masse and dislodge it after only a few seconds.

Sunday, 2 November

The camp teenage boy is talking to his companion on the bus: "I can tell he's got a crush on me but if I say owt I know he's just gonna say, 'I'm not gay!' in that stupid indignant voice".

Behind me, the grey-haired hi-vis man has been to the new restaurant that apparently everybody is talking about: "I ordered the lamb but when it came

it was all fat. I got one tiny thin slice of meat off the whole piece! I sent it back. I can't eat that I said, it's all fat. The woman asked me, 'Do you want to order something else?' I said, 'No love, you've put me right off my tea now, I'm going home to make myself some beans on toast.' The chef chased me out into the car park and told me he was going to have word with the butcher but I'll not be going back".

I walk down Leeds Road behind a girl in skinny jeans and a black puffer jacket. She's talking loudly on her phone in Polish, emphasising key points with wild, histrionic hand gestures.

There's a woman in the Costcutter with 'Nobody's Cow' appliquéd onto her onesie above her breasts. Outside, the man with the piercings is polishing the alloys of his Ford Fiesta with one hand while he smokes some strong weed with the other. He smiles and waves.

Out in the sticks, it's all long shadows, wood smoke and lavender, starlings on wires, church bells, dried hydrangeas, Kate Bush songs from the open windows of ex farm buildings, wicker-baskets, wellington boots, a possible sighting of a small flock of waxwings and a definite sighting of a huge flock of lapwings.

There are plastic bags in the trees.

I was nearly hit twice by flying objects today: I had to swerve to avoid the soiled nappy that somebody threw from their front door towards the bins without looking, then at the farm I had to duck under the flight path of an enraged goose. It hissed and honked and flew over the five bar gate at me in a rage. The old farmer ran out and got himself between the goose and me, flapping his arms at it, "It's a right little bastard this 'en!" he explained, as he tried to shepherd it back into the yard, "It dun't like me either—keeps biting me. It's never flown ovva t'gate before though!"

Saturday, 15 November

6.15am: Dancers and bouncers share jokes and cigarettes outside the strip club. The dancers are wearing their 'standing outside' uniform: white faux-mink coats, suspenders and heels. The bouncers wear black suits and patent shoes.

The man behind me on the bus to the hospital has a loud hacking cough. I get off where a group of builders with hard hats over their hoods are smoking in a huddle outside the house with the empty Cheese Curls packet and the pile of dog shit underneath the trampoline in the yard.

There's a lot of rotten pre-recession *Ground Force* decking around here and it's slippery and treacherous at this time of year; the old man with butter on his nose advised me to watch myself after I slipped on his.

In the street, a young man with a shaved head and tracksuit is vacuuming his brand new Vauxhall Corsa while he listens to Robbie Williams quite loudly.

Out in the sticks, beyond where the remains of the smashed up traffic cone have been strewn across the road for weeks. Beyond even where the empty breakfast bowl and spoon have been left on top of the dry-stone wall a half mile from the nearest house (It's been there for several days and there's an inch-and-a-half of rainwater in the bowl now), a low mist is sitting in the valley bottom. The grey road is accented with orange cherry leaves and a large flock of fieldfares is messily stripping out all the berries from a big rowan tree.

On the driveway at Oakwood, a man of about thirty-five, with a beard and donkey jacket, has his head under the bonnet of his thirty-year-old Saab 900 while he listens to Talking Heads quite loudly.

Sunday, 7 December

Every day this week, I've seen the lonely pig on the moor. It runs to the perimeter of its pen and stares at me as I walk past. Yesterday morning, when it came to meet me, I made two pig-like grunts (I don't know why, I wasn't really thinking about it) and it responded in exactly the same manner.

Further up the moor, Mr Briggs pulls up. He winds down the window of his Suzuki Carry and tells me that he and his missus have been by coach to Eastbourne for a 'Turkey and Tinsel Weekender'. "Aye," he explains, "Tuesday was Christmas Eve, Wednesday was Christmas Day, and Thursday was New Year's Day. £125-a-head all-in—including four drinks, which is enough. We had a real time!" Mr Briggs goes on to tell me that by the Thursday (New Year's Day) he'd found he fancied a fish. He says he travelled to a chip shop in Brighton only to find that they cost £10.50 so he hadn't bothered in the end.

Back in town, the gas board are digging up the roads. The woman in the pink onesie, who is sitting on her front step surrounded by small statues of Yorkshire terriers while she smokes a cigarette, tells me "It's a right pain, there's nowhere to bloody park."

A gold Kia Picanto screeches to a halt outside the church and a man in his seventies with a beard and glasses gets out brandishing a small hand plane. He slams shut the car door, shoulders open the gate of the churchyard and sprints down the path and through the open doors. Within seconds I can hear the sound of wood being energetically smoothed echoing out from the church interior.

At 2.30pm, at the top of the hill, I encounter two large women in their seventies. They are dressed in identical spotted Dalmatian onesies and appear to be very drunk. They cling to one another as they zig-zag across the middle of the road whilst inexplicably making load "miaow" noises like enormous bipedal dog-cats.

In the supermarket, the woman with the sensible shoes and bag-for-life is telling her husband about her dislike of Milk Tray chocolates. "Don't ever buy me Milk Tray again! I hate them! Joan bought me some last year and I've still got them. Yuk!"

Monday, 22 December

The sun is low, boiler flues are pluming, the garden gate is slimy, and the old man with the eye-patch, bandana, boot-cut jeans and biker jacket is bemoaning "All this bloody rigmarole for £1.63 in bloody pension credits" to his neighbour, the tall thin man in the plastic reindeer antlers with the dew-drop hanging from his nose.

All of a sudden hailstones are bouncing off the 'Santa, Please Stop Here' sign which is planted in the pot next to the fake plastic topiary bay tree.

A woman with an anorak and a bag-for-life is talking to a group of other women with bags-for-life. "I don't feel the cold anymore because I've got…" she stops to think for a moment, then turns to the woman in the enormous scarf next to her, "What is it I've got, Joyce?" "Diabetes," says Joyce. "No!" says the woman, suddenly remembering, "A onesie."

Sunday, 13 January 2015

The buses are racing each other between stops. The world flies past the window in a blur: BEST CARPET BARGAINS… Klippers Hair Salon… Sambuca Saturday… Karaoke Thursday… MEGA BOXES FOR £8.99… Royal Travel and Money Transfer… iTaste… Extra Care Housing… 2 For 1 on Essentials (illustrated with a photograph of a packet of digestive biscuits)… YOU CAN'T BUY CHEAPER… Gold International… LE

UVST TIPE X… FREE BOTTLE OF POP. A man climbs aboard looking flustered in fake leather and Fair Isle, "It's always bloody late, this bus! He's supposed to be five minutes in front of that other one", he says out loud as he walks down the aisle. "Bloody rubbish!" He sits down next to me in a fug of damp and sweat. The woman in front of us with the grey perm and turquoise gaberdine coat turns around, "These people are much more helpful than the Metro people though", she says, "And it's 30p cheaper", she adds, her knuckles white on the handrail as the bus swings out into the middle lane to overtake its rival. "Go on, lad!" yells the damp sweat man to the driver, pumping his fist.

A pride of door-to-door salesmen (beards, short-back-and-sides, black bomber jackets, black too-long-in-the-leg trousers, black winkle-picker shoes, black zip-up briefcases) are gobbing on the floor and vaping outside the Costcutter. I pass them on my way to the terrace of houses where, during the course of the last twenty-five years, the sheds, the painted lintels, the hebes and hawthorne, the privet and the pyracantha, the decorative limestone and calcite have all been replaced with soiled nappies, empty Skips packets, sundry broken pieces of board (mainly hard and chip) sodden underwear, empty milk cartons, a football boot, a stained mattress, empty paint tins, a broken toothbrush, a dustpan, a bent trampoline on its side, assorted lengths of polythene, a broken monster truck toy, party-popper shells, broken bottles, rusty pieces of micro-scooter, bits of an old gate, dog shit, traffic cones, energy drink cans, a kitchen unit with mould on it, a car with lichen on it, takeaway trays and a partially incinerated (artificial) Christmas tree.

The woman in the faded pink anorak and Nike trainers is talking on the phone as she gets off the bus. "I got her some One Direction perfume… I know!

Me neither. I'm going to put it away for her for next Christmas… It was only a tenner… You can't go wrong, can you? And it's lovely and fruity—I'd wear it. Those princess ones she has are vile… I don't know… Horrible… Yeah, just as a stocking filler… perfect… I know! Lovely and fruity, I'd wear it— much nicer than these princess ones… Yeah… only a tenner… I know… One Direction perfume for only a tenner, it's not to be sniffed at…"

Sunday, 25 January

The snow on the tops is striped with icy 4x4 tracks. It's laid thick and muffles both the early wood-pigeon call and the shouts from the high school football match: hi-vis vests and a hi-vis ball.

The man with the dewdrop on his nose is polishing his Jaguar XJ. He lives in a park-home on the moor. He has one of those old ding-dong doorbells (black plastic box with a solid, reliable button that looks like a sun-bleached Trebor Refresher) that are more usually found at the big houses with the heated driveways further down the valley. The man tells me his neighbours have fallen out with him. "They're jealous since I got the Jag", he says, "Them over your left shoulder… Don't look!" he says, without taking his eyes off mine, "They'll know we're talking about them. They complain every time I step out of the house. And them over my left shoulder, they rang the council because I took my dog out without a lead!" I glance down at the floor and kick a chipping of the decorative spar back behind the concrete rope-edging in an attempt to look nonchalant in front of the neighbours, and he continues, "I don't know why we can't all just get on, I bet we sound like a load of school kids, don't we? But we're all pensioners!"

Later, In the garden of the man who hasn't put his teeth in yet, I see a ring-necked parakeet in the cherry tree.

In the garden opposite, a large and rowdy flock of black-headed gulls is squabbling over something on the lawn. The man without his teeth says they frightened him when he first come outside, "It's like that Alfred Hitchcock film" he says, "You know the one I mean?" "*The Birds*?" I say. "Aye, that's the one. Let's just hope Michael's not lying dead behind that hedge."

Tuesday, 24 February

Things are slowly drying out in the first real sun of the year. Snowdrops and crocuses are appearing on the verges. The big woman in a dirty pink onesie on the bench at the side of the main road inhales from her cigarette with her eyes closed. She adjusts her posture, unfurling like an enormous pink fleecy rose, stretching out her arms across the backrest. She tilts her head back to absorb the warmth of the sun on her face and exhales a long thin wisp of white smoke vertically up and over Lockwood Taxis.

Across the road, an old man in synthetic fibres rustles past the upturned push-chair. The sun has yet to coax him from his tightly secured drawstring hood despite its low glare turning his Reactolite lenses black, opaque. His vision must be impaired because he almost bumps into the woman in the grey hooded top, black tracksuit pants and enormous pink fluffy slippers as she comes out of the off-licence.

The estate is a spiky forest of broken saplings and TV aerials, where puddles reflect lowered hatchbacks and the dogs bark all day long. Somebody has drawn a half-arsed cock-and-balls motif in biro on the postman's pouch box. Half-a-dozen scruffy men on pit bikes systematically doorstep the residents: "Alright, love? Just wondering if you've owt for scrap? Okay, love... Sorry, darling... Right, love..." A knackered white Transit follows in their wake, pausing outside the house with the bright blue plastic hanging baskets either side of the moulded Ionic columns in filthy, chipped UPVC. One of the pit bike men has discovered an old car tyre on the drive. He opens the Transit's back doors and chucks it in.

Out on Hangingstone Road, a couple of workmen appear to be dismantling the CCTV gantry that sometimes gets mail addressed to it (On two occasions now, I have come across mail addressed to the CCTV Camera, Hangingstone Road, Huddersfield).

Friday, 13 March

A shoal of jackdaws swells overhead as the line of geese that are scouring the field off Storthes Hall Lane edge forward in unison like policemen in overalls conducting a fingertip search.

Ten years ago, the pair of plastic ornamental bay trees either side of the front door of the house on the moor were quite an authentic 'bay' green, but now they have faded and bleached to a kind of washed-out 'toothpaste' turquoise. In the garden, Mr Walker is making the most of the mild weather and is carrying out some maintenance. He has balanced the frost-severed head of the stone tortoise on top of a statuette of a baby rabbit. The head has thereby been raised to a height and angle that has allowed Mr Walker to realign it with its headless body and to create the illusion that the tortoise is still whole. I can hardly see the join. The result is a touching tableau in which the tortoise appears to be glancing over the baby rabbit's back to keep a weather eye out for predators.

The temperature is into double figures, shag pile moss covers the top-stones, there's not a cloud in the sky and the man in the heavy duffle coat with the hood up wants to know what the hell it is I think I'm doing.

"Come in! Come in!" shouts the old man at the manor house on the moor as I approach the door, "I hear you've grown a beard!" he says, mistaking me for somebody else.

A woman in a little hat with netty bits waves to me from a Rolls Royce.

Thursday, 19 March

Sunlight streams through gaps in the clouds, dramatically spotlighting both the Emley Moor mast and Mr Hussain's plastic lawn. The past few weeks have seen Mr Hussain's fake lawn divided into a series of rectangular strips by the long Mohicans of real lawn that have breached its seams.

Next door, a big gold two-litre Mercedes is blocking the pavement. I walk around it while the jackdaws squabble noisily on a chimney pot overhead. There are four stone urns in a neat row below the big picture window, three of which are topped with a stone sphere. The fourth has a weathered, regulation size Mitre football substitute.

The houses on this estate haven't changed much since they were built in the early 1970s: a series of brick semis with postage-stamp lawns bordered with daffodils and primulas. The cul-de-sac is lined all the way to the turning circle with regularly spaced identical 'feature' bay windows, glazed with stick-on leaded lights. The wooden, approximately Doric architraves are rotting now and several have been replaced with moulded UPVC—as have many of the windows and doors—but all the brass reproduction Victorian stagecoach lamps have been retained. There's evidence of the original concrete road surface through scars in the asphalt too.

Audi, Audi, Ford Mondeo, Mercedes, Kia, Land Rover and, on the five-bar gated driveway at the bottom, underneath the leylandii that has been precision topiaried to accommodate it, a pristine, twelve-year-old Rover 75 Tourer in metallic red.

There's nobody on the streets around here except for old women at bus stops and the occasional commercial dog walker. A Toyota Yaris goes past leaving a trail of weed smoke in its wake.

Friday, 27 March

On the estate where people in bathrobes often shout loudly at barking dogs above the noise of high-energy auto-tuned pop, they are shouting particularly loudly today. The wind whistles through the streets, slamming knackered garden gates, flapping and cracking at the polythene in the broken trees and inducing that weird clanging sound from the inside of metal street lamps. A man of about sixty years old in a tracksuit and an old Suzuki Swift pulls over to ask me whether I know where he was born. I say I don't. "Sorry, I mean, the thing is, my wife asked me where I was born the other day and I realised I don't know. My mum's dead, so I can't ask her so I sent off for my birth certificate and it says Storths Road but I don't know where that is."

I can hear a woodpecker in the tree above the owl that's made of hundreds of tiny shells.

An elderly man in a stained anorak is sitting on an upturned bucket to paint his garden fence. He tells me he used to work for the GPO, "...on the engineering side, like. I've got a good pension. It's seen me right! I've been retired for twenty-eight years. I bet it's not like that anymore though, is it? I couldn't believe it when they privatised the Royal Mail; nobody wanted it! It was all just to line the pockets of the big boys. Greedy buggers". He dips his brush into the paint, "It's water based, this" he points out. I comment on the unpredictable weather we've been having. "Aye, but isn't it grand working outside? I love it. I always have. I think it's why I'm so fit—apart from me knees, and me back. I've always worked outside. It

can be the worst job in the world but as long as you're outside and you've got some good workmates it doesn't matter." I agree with him, and tell him about my back and knee problems. He sympathises and then parks his brush. "I'm going to call it a do for today", he says, groping for a dry bit of fence to pull himself upright. "I've enjoyed our chat. It makes the world go round, doesn't it? Talking to folk? But there're some right miseries around these days, aren't there? My bus driver says he hates his job because everybody's so miserable now."

Three doors down, a tall man in a black anorak and sandals is looking directly ahead and holding his hands behind his back as he paces slowly round and round the perimeter of the small concreted-over garden of his terrace house.

Tuesday, 7 April

Woman at the back of the bus in a three-quarter length quilted anorak: "You should have seen us roller skating the other night!" Other woman in three-quarter length quilted anorak: "You weren't kaylied as you were going round, were you?" Woman in three-quarter length quilted anorak: "Aye, the drunker we got, the braver we got."

Crisp shadows, blue sky, a starting of blossom with the shreds of newspaper in the trees, a weathered, grey wooden fence with the greenest cotoneaster leaking through the cracks, the second bullfinch in a week on Newsome Road South, rotten gates that fall apart in your hand, a moulded 'stone' tortoise with a solar panel shell and a night-light face, massive cars parked too close together, a woven willow reindeer which is still kicking around from Christmas…

Mr Briggs pulls over in his Suzuki Carry. He takes his pipe out of his mouth and pins it between the ball of his thumb and the steering wheel while he leans

across and shouts to me through the window: "I'm off to t'bins; I've got a load of bloody rubbish in!" And he drives away.

I see Mr Eagle outside the newsagent's. He tells me again about the time he went to see The Rolling Stones in 1980: "Mick Jagger was from me to where that Renault's parked... Jill was on my shoulders... The car broke down on the way home..."

Saturday, 18 April

A still day: petrol, cigarette smoke, lawn-mowers, paper litter, traffic noises from a quarter-mile away, daisies, dandelions and daffodils, a peacock butterfly on white UPVC...

Out on the estate that hasn't changed for forty years, the old couple are having a small tiff about which bag to put all those jam jars in while a sparrowhawk disembowels a small rodent on the ridge of their dormer bungalow.

Rockeries, cracked-flag driveways, scuffed casey footballs, bikes on their sides, tiny weed-bound ponds, bird feeders, overweight builders with broad accents, 8x8' lawns, cotoneasters, hebes, leylandii, a willow or a silver birch in the corner—planted by the developer in the seventies—low double-skinned fake-sandstone walls infilled with soil and alpines, brutal pruning, and a David Brown tractor spreading muck on the field behind.

There are lots of large women in their fifties and sixties with grown-out grey bobs, Reactolite glasses, floral shirts—sometimes open with a pastel vest-top underneath—and knee-length shorts, also in pastel. They sit sipping gin & slim outside the pub waiting for "probably the best fish supper in town".

The chickens in the field full of mangold wurzels are excited, they sound as though they are singing Khachaturian's 'Sabre Dance'. I hear lapwings, buzzards,

and the nearly naked man walking the Border terrier who is singing at the top of his voice.

Saturday, 23 May

I leave at 6am and the low sun is glinting off silver seams of slug trail. At the junction where the double yellow lines divert around the big sycamore, Jackson Pollock bird shit covers the road and part of the abandoned pushchair.

A funfair has set up in the park, behind the row of massive Dolly Mixture holly bushes. I walk past behind two other men in high-vis vests: "Do you know that guy up Deighton with one arm?" "Stumpy?" "Aye, that's him, Stumpy…"

In town, I pass a noisy lock-in at the bar under the railway arches: 'Setting the new standard of late night drinking culture…'

I drive out into the country, where nightclub moguls and ex-football professionals have built big houses as high up the panoramic ridge as possible. They compete for the stripiest lawns, the most striking life-sized Buddhas, the shiniest black 4x4s, the most unorthodox use of decorative gravels and spars etc.

Mr Briggs pulls up in an old Toyota Yaris. "I've just taxed this: £60. Just insured it: £250." That's all. And he drives away again.

In the village, this year's flying ant day is underway and the builders are listening to eighties heavy metal on a paint-spattered radio.

Back in town, a man with a chin-strap beard pops up from behind the fence of the residential care home: "Hello, mate. Do you know me?" he asks. "No," I say. "Well, this is a residential home and I'm Wayne. I'm a bit autistic; I'm always thinking people are going to knife me. That's no way to carry on, is it?" "No", I say, and then add, "You should be all right at the moment, there's nobody around", and I set off walking again. Wayne shouts after me, "But I look all right though, don't I?" I shout back, "Yeah, yes, you look fine!"

Saturday, 6 June

The postman leans against the bus shelter and squints into the squall, "As long as my fags and my phone are dry, I don't give a shit about anything else", he says.

Two ducks fly over the swathes of buttercups in the yellow meadow off Moor Lane.

"Are burglars poor?" the young son asks his dad. "That depends on how successful a burglar they are", his dad replies.

A pair of crows fly over the Ferrari, the rhododendrons and the brace of Range Rovers. They land on the ridge tiles of Wisteria Cottage with its gravel, its vintage boot jack, the stone pixies climbing over its gate, and its wisteria.

The views, the cars and the houses around here, are massive.

There's an angry bee trapped under the plastic envelope that's housing the planning notice stuck to the lamp post next to the Toyota Previa with the long deliberate looking scratch down its side.

The man from Sunny View has come outside, his hood drawstring tight. He tells me to get myself out of the rain.

I wonder if the little ginger dog turd left next to the imprint of a dog's paw in the cement around the drain cover is a memorial tribute.

The old lady with the piles of books and the oxygen tank has died.

The couple who are always arguing with the windows open are arguing with the windows open.

"Nice one, mate. See you later, bud", says the young man through a haze of weed smoke from the passenger seat of the little Suzuki Ignis with the Ferrari air freshener hanging from the rearview mirror.

The sun dries the rain and brings out the man in the shorts who hoovers his pattern imprinted concrete driveway. The man in the rugby shirt calls his Jack Russell terrier a knobhead and a tit.

The man in his seventies with the opaque Reactolites and the black Labrador stops to talk to the other man in his seventies with opaque Reactolites and black Labrador. They compare their experiences of electrocardiography.

The roofers' expletive ridden conversation is easily loud enough to be heard from the bus stop where the woman with the Sainsbury's bag-for-life raises an outraged eyebrow.

What I thought was a bee in the pocket of my shirt was just a piece of leaf litter.

The estate agent in the tailored grey waistcoat, jeans, light tan brogues and sunglasses climbs out of his black Audi S4. He grabs the large, strappy digital SLR from the passenger seat, takes a couple of snaps of the end-terrace with the pretend wooden front door and drives away again.

Back in town, I get off the bus where the Asian man who is wearing salwar kameez and holding a toilet seat is having a stand-up row about parking spaces with a fat bald white man with no shirt on and ketchup around his mouth.

Wednesday, 17th June

Litter Survey, Fitzwilliam Street to Church Street, via Greenhead Park, Heaton Road, and Branch Street: Costa take-out cup, Coca-Cola plastic bottle, Mayfair cigarette packet, Greggs take-out plastic cup, Richmond cigarette packet, Greggs take-out paper bag, Benson & Hedges cigarette packet, Kinder Bueno packaging, train ticket, 7up drink can, pile of indeterminate cigarette butts, Coca-Cola plastic bottle, polystyrene takeaway container, Dairy Milk wrapper, Haribo sweet packet, Benson & Hedges cigarette packet, Wheat Crunchies packet, Richmond cigarette packet, Rizla packaging, Kellogs Coco Pops Snack Bar wrapper, Ribena plastic bottle, Benson & Hedges cigarette packet, Benson & Hedges cigarette packet, expired DVLA tax disc, Capri Sun carton, till receipt, pages from The Huddersfield Examiner, polystyrene cup, Capri Sun carton, two 'wet wipes', a child's seaside fishing net, Mayfair cigarette packet (20), Mayfair cigarette packet (10), pile of indeterminate cigarette butts, Coca-Cola can, Costa sugar wrapper, Boost Energy Drink can, Pepsi can, Maoam sweet wrapper, Mr Freeze packaging, Rubicon mango drink can, Walkers Cheese & Onion crisps, Mayfair cigarette packet, plastic fork, polystyrene cup, polystyrene cup, paper serviette, plastic water bottle (indeterminate brand), a hair roller, Snickers wrapper, Lucozade bottle, Wrigley's Extra chewing gum wrapper, Paracodol packaging, Lambert & Butler cigarette packet.

Sunday, 21 June

In the close humidity of snapped off saplings, broken concrete, takeaway flyers, footballs in trees and trainers on wires, the dirty scrap man with the homemade tattoos is here for the Ikea bedstead.

Two teens with half-closed eyes smoke weed while their Staffy intimidates the old woman in salwar kameez.

The shop is stuffy and smells of dog food. A young woman buys four bottles of Fruit Shoot, "I water them down but he still acts like a wild child, It's a bloody nightmare!"

Further up the valley, in the open breeze and swaying beech trees, the Abel & Cole man buzzes around the laburnum, rhododendron, and the topiary box

footballs in his tidy fleece jacket and yellow van.

The council gardener is sitting on the kerb mixing up some two-stroke in a jerry can while his colleague is on his knees lifting out dandelions at the base of the school fence.

A man walking a Cairn terrier passes me, "Are you lost?" he asks.

Friday, 10 July

On the estate where pretend owls outnumber the human population by two to one, there have been some new editions: a tiny motorbike-and-side-car with solar powered head-lamps, a concrete kitten, a miniature pretend stone elephant—curled up asleep, lots of new meerkats and Buddhas and an entire garden stocked exclusively with faded plastic flora and fauna. The underlying murmur of people in tight shorts commenting on the warm weather to one another all day long is occasionally punctuated with the noise of power tools and the yelping of small dogs. And, over by the abandoned Renault Camper, a man in his seventies is showing his new teddy bear to the woman with pictures of wolves on her t-shirt.

Further up the valley, outside the High School, the road sweeping man picks up Maoam wrappers with an extendable litter-picker while his soft toy trophy-lynchings swing from the handle of his cart.

The fine weather has brought out the clover, the daisies, the bird's foot trefoil, the mother-die, buttercups, foxgloves, honeysuckle, and the old woman with her specs on a chain who shuffles past a pile of dried dog shit in her open-toed sandals.

Out in the sticks, a hen pheasant flaps out from under the five bar gate at the bottom of the field with the old bathtub in it, and a Porsche 4x4 blows past with its windows open, trailing aftershave.

Outside the village hall, there are pots of marigolds around the old church pew with chintz cushions. There's ivy, there are climbing roses, yew hedges, willow and birch. There are gravel paths with moss edging, potted geraniums and snap-dragons. There are spaniels and Labradors, and pairs of upside-down gardening shoes covered in lawn clippings. There is best bitter, and Radio 4, and Botox, and swallows and martins in the outhouses. Happy golfers wave me past the tee where the stolen top-stones have already been replaced.

It starts to rain summer rain, fat drops that leave big Dalmatian spots on the millstone flags. At the big house with the yellow lichen gables, the old man with the comb-over and frayed grey flannels is frustrated, "I've just come out to do a bit in the garden and bugger me if it hasn't started raining".

At the modernist house that is being extended using mainly large sheets of chipboard, the builders are discussing an episode of *Top Gear* in voices that carry. "Wasn't it funny when that caravan tried to overtake on the inside—on that bumpy bit?" "You think we have a good laugh at work; imagine being them!"

A woman walks past with a big Siberian husky, then a jogger who is going barely fast enough to overtake her—he's wiping the rain from his glasses with the hem of his Scotland football shirt.

The old woman at the farm asks whether I've got a mac in my van. I say I have and she gives me a double thumbs up and a big grin, "Well, go and put it on, I can see the blobs all over your shirt!"

Back in town, the woman with the long-haired dachshunds is talking to the man taking photographs from the viewing point in the park. "It's gorgeous, isn't it? Yes," says the man "We don't appreciate it enough, living round here, do we?"

Sunday, 2 August

The black liner of the wire litter bin outside the Costcutter has blown inside-out in the wind and is flapping about inflated like a smaller, less cocksure, banana and ketchup-stained version of the promotional 'air-dancers' they used to have outside the Fiat garage when it was a Peugeot one.

A delivery van pulls up and the driver gets out. While he's unloading fruit and veg' he explains how he'd earlier mistaken his own reflection in his misaligned nearside wing mirror for another person and, in the resulting confusion had almost crashed his van into a wall.

The Kia saloon with the office chair and the postcard display rack strapped to its roof drives past me in the same place it did yesterday.

When the old man who was cleaning his immaculate twelve-year-old Ford Mondeo initially engaged me in conversation, I'd assumed he was just being friendly to a stranger, but when he asked me a technical question about the tactics employed by the Huddersfield Giants at their last game, I wondered whether he had mistaken me for somebody else. Not being much of a fan of rugby league, I confessed I had no idea what he was talking about. At first the man looked confused but then he smiled, got up from where he'd been crouching to polish the chrome of his vintage AA radiator grill badge, and persisted with the subject—presumably assuming I was just amusing myself by teasing him. I reasserted my ignorance on the matter and voiced my suspicion that I wasn't who he thought I was. Once more, the man briefly looked confused, nervously wrapping his duster around his hand, but again he smiled and continued on the subject. As he seemed so convinced I was somebody I wasn't, I began to doubt myself; perhaps we had met before and

I'd forgotten. Maybe he'd brought up the Huddersfield Giants in conversation on that occasion too and I'd somehow given him the impression that I had some interest and knowledge on the subject—It could easily happen during the course of small talk in a queue or on a bus. I decided to go with this scenario and explained that while I do like to keep an eye on the Giants' results, I don't consider myself to be much of an expert and have no worthwhile opinion on their tactics. At this, the man smiled, raised his hands to his eyes like blinkers and said conspiratorially, "I know! It's all claret and gold with some people, isn't it?" At this point, we were interrupted by the two builders who were sitting side-by-side on some scaffolding while they chiselled render from the house next door. They had begun singing R Kelly's 'I Believe I Can Fly' at the tops of their voices. The old man looked up and shouted over, "Give it a rest now lads!" but it had no effect.

Further down the road I got talking to the woman with the low maintenance hairstyle and the perhaps inadvisable vest top with no bra. She was telling me about the house she used to live in when she was younger. "Where was that?" I asked. She waved an enormous arm in the vague direction of half of Huddersfield and said, "You know, number 23 do-dah".

On, and up past the quarry, the airfield, the firework factory and the caravan park to the cul-de-sac of neat 1960s bungalows where the sound of *Woman's Hour* is leaking from open kitchen windows and the air smells of freshly cut leylandii. There's talk of chimineas: "Good grief, how many of these are we having?"

The doctors' surgery is empty apart from an elderly woman and an elderly man who are staring impassively at different walls at either end of the waiting room while 'Lessons in Love' by Level 42 plays through the discreetly mounted speakers at quite a high volume.

Wednesday, 19 August

6am: It's quiet on the street apart from the man in the black tracksuit who is singing an indefinable song quite loudly outside Ali Barber's barber shop.

10am: In town, the old woman in the open-toed sandals is waiting to cross the road outside the supermarket with her Inca inspired bag-for-life. Next to her is a younger man in a pink shirt and a red, yellow, green and black striped Rasta cap. They cross the road together and make their way around the pile of rubble that was, until last week, the old university sports hall. They pass a soberly dressed man at the bus stop— shiny black shoes, grey suit trousers, pale pink shirt—who is drinking a can of extra strength lager.

11.30am: In the suburbs, the asphalt is melting. The sun is out, the hydrangeas are out, the big men in shorts and flip-flops are out. A swarm of bees has taken up residence in a crack in the wall of the contract weaver's shed and the man in the leather gauntlets says "All right, mate?" to me outside the shop that sells mainly tinned peas, jars of tuna paste, and extra-strength cider. My old school teacher has moved house and the new owner has paved over the garden and replaced the big old gloss black hard-wood door and leaded lights with white UPVC. There has also been a prolifera-tion of CND graffiti around here recently.

12.30pm: The knackered old boat that I sometimes park up behind for cover while I have a quick brew, is gone. I ask the man who is pouring some concrete where it is. He says I've just missed it, "Some blokes have been to tow it away." Around the corner, I see it, stationary and listing badly in the middle of the road, one of the wheels has fallen off its trailer.

3pm: At the shop, the man in front of me in the queue asks for an e-cigarette charger. The proprietor ducks behind the counter, rummages around, and comes back up with a USB phone charger. "No" says the man, "It's for my e-cigarettes". The proprietor disappears into a storeroom and returns with a large plastic box. He sits it on the counter and pulls out three or four different USB phone chargers. "No", says the man, "It's for my e-cigarettes; you know, a three pin plug for the mains with a bit that you screw onto the cigarette at the other end". The proprietor rummages through the box again and pulls out another USB phone charger. "I tell you what", says the man, "Give me twenty Chesterfield Lights". The proprietor rolls up the shutter to the tobacco cabinet, takes out a packet of twenty JPS and puts them on the counter with all the phone cables. "No", says the man, "20 Chesterfield Lights. There, bottom left". The proprietor replaces the packet of JPS and returns with a packet of JPS Blue. "No", says the man, "I tell you what, Give me 20 Rothmans Superkings, right in the middle there". The proprietor replaces the JPS Blue, takes out the Rothmans and hands them over. "Thank you", says the man.

Friday, 4 September

A cyclist with squeaky brakes and a pair of crutches strapped to his back passes me as I walk into work.

On the bus with some other men in high visibility clothing, the main topics of conversation are caravans, caravan based holidays, and the football transfer window. I alight at the nursing home and follow the woman on the mobility scooter past the ivy-covered lampposts, the pink hydrangeas, the smeared dog shit and the sandwich packaging. I turn off along the terrace with no front gardens; a long row of telly backs and cable knots. I turn off again to a stinking dog piss accreted yard of crisp packets, expanding foam, dandelions and empty milk cartons next door to an obsessive mini Versaille of hoverflies, succulents and fancy gravels. The clock tower strikes the hour and the running man with the dog jumps over the spilt grab bag of Maltesers; neat parallel rows of chocolate beads line up in the grate of the storm drain. Out from the tidy side street of bungalows, the ladies begin to flock with their hair set, their trouser suits pressed, their shoes gold and their shopping bags for life. They each round the corner into the main road and get a wet slap in the face from the big overhanging buddleia. I carry on past the sheltered houses with their gladioli in planters, beige washing lines and handwritten No Parking signs. On, past the back-to-backs where the dock leaves grow from the thick green snail-slime striated moss on the stone steps below the leaky guttering. Past the fairy lights and decking, the cooking sauce jars, squashed slugs and blackberries. On up to the new estate with the fake bricked-up windows, the concrete lintels and architraves, the pretend leaded lights, the miniature gardens (where the box shrubs have already overstepped their boundaries) and the herringbone paving in the communal parking bays: a small Honda, a large Honda, an Astra a Citroen C1… I cut across the sodden plastic lawn (laid directly over stone flags) to the big, gated Victorian, Atkinson Grimshaw mansions whose wide-as-a-street driveways are bordered with poplar, rhododendron, holly, begonia, topiary teddy bears, ferns and golden beech leaves on neatly trimmed lawns; the first fall of autumn. The only other person around is the happy old man with the walking frame.

Monday, 21 September

A heron flies over Dale Cottage and the last of its pink fuchsias. On the driveway, the man in the blue Vauxhall Zafira with

the ladders on the roof is listening to Sigala at high volume. He rocks back and forth enthusiastically in the driver's seat, mouthing the words, ecstatic.

In the 'Best Kept Village' that smells of two-stroke chainsaw oil, the houses are never finished. The builders have moved on a generation. Out have gone those firms, traditionally named after their proprietor, whose contractors have broad Yorkshire accents, gold earrings and eighties hits on their site radios: 'Don't You Want Me, Baby?' And in have come the firms named after a single word synonym for 'house': Home, Abode, Dwelling, Base etc. whose contractors have tattoo sleeves, full-face beards, and nineties hits on their site radios: 'A Design For Life'.

At the big house in the woods, one of the modern, nineties builders is hoovering the pattern imprinted concrete driveway while another spreads a smelly solvent sealer onto it with a yard brush.

At the house with the big view, the woman in the bathrobe is talking to her neighbour, the man in the lumber-jack shirt who has retired to make chainsaw carvings of owls to sell at country art fairs. Her as yet unrecon-structed builder, is up a ladder carrying out some never-ending repairs while listening to a histrionic heavy rock guitar solo from about 1986: 'Livin' on a Prayer'. "I had the pheasant and Richard had the grouse", the woman explains, "It was really nicely cooked. Really nice. Lovely".

Sunday, 4 October

The man sitting two seats in front of me on the bus is wearing 1980s suit trousers, a beige anorak, and some-thing that looks like bird shit in his hair. He's repeatedly slapping himself about the head and face. Behind me, the self-important man in corduroy is begging to differ with the woman with the bag-for-life, "It's not! It's

gonna be another sodding Chinese! Why we need another sodding Chinese when there's already one at the bloody bottom I don't know!" he says before going on to explain that he's given up drinking. The woman looks sceptical.

The weather has turned over the last few weeks and they're selling Christmas decorations at Sainsbury's and Morrison's. The dry cleaner on the ring-road is offering a 'Seasonal Ugg Boot Cleaning Service'.

On the moor, acorns and oak leaves litter the pavement next to the beagles' kennels. There's shattered green glass in the gutter. There are concrete lampposts (Concrete Utilities Ltd), GPO manhole covers, and a pile of dead wood behind an ivy-covered wall. There are ferns and holly, rose hips, barking dogs, and cawing crows in the tops of the trees. The house with the half-dozen muddy turnips on the doorstep is being clad in pretend wood.

At the bottom end of the estate, driveways are being resurfaced with small pebbles suspended in clear resin which make them look kind of edible. There are plastic lawns too, and rusty super-minis, and Octavia Hackney carriages. There are new plastic storm drain grates and concrete top-stones to replace the stolen originals.

At the top of the estate, among the big detached houses, there are leylandii, succulents, rockeries and Alpines, some big toadstools that weren't there yesterday, a beech hedge, a big overhanging silver birch, ornamental lampposts, pretend mailboxes that are actually bird boxes, yellow grit bins, water butts, high maintenance borders, patios, 'Burglars Beware' neighbourhood watch signs, fire hydrants, bird baths, sundials, and vibrant hi-visibility moss in the grikes between the expensive driveway setts. There's a power cut and all the burglar alarms go off at once.

Wednesday, 21 October

Autumn morning: headlights, street-lights, a pile of bakers' trays outside the corner shop, students taking photos of leaves.

On the bus, the man in front of me says that café culture is wasted on him because he doesn't drink tea or coffee. He goes on to explain that he could never eat Weetabix without sugar.

At the supermarket, the woman with the piercings and leggings is complaining because the Festive Yard of Scrumptious Jaffa Cakes Christmas Pack she's bought is "just a long box with some normal packets of Jaffa Cakes inside".

I turn the radio on and a woman is talking about leaving her son to get himself to university on his own because she had to go and visit her energy master in Bali. I turn it over and a man is singing the lyric "She maxed her credit cards and don't got a job" to the tune of a Duran Duran song. I turn it off again.

The blind man with the green hi-vis coat and white stick is tip-tapping the high stone wall as he makes his way from the bus stop towards the hospital. He nimbly rounds a couple of junction boxes and a litter bin before walking face first into the larger-than-life-sized white-stick-defying pedestal-mounted Clear Channel hoarding promoting SlimFast Slim-Taki™ Noodles: 'DATE NIGHT FRIDAY Chop-chop'.

Sunday, 1 November

Storm drains are overflowing. An empty packet of Lambert & Butler and an energy drink can overtake me in the swollen run-off channel at the side of the road.

In the big yellow cherry tree, starlings make noises like excited children on a coach trip.

A Jack Russell terrier escapes from the woman with the mid-calf length floral print pleated skirt and the summer wine perm, and chases the Land Rover as it reverses into the driveway. "Stupid bloody dog!" says the woman, "It's his boss that's come back. That's what's done it!" she explains.

The flats with the pretentious name smell like a swimming pool today.

The man in the long overcoat is reading a book and drinking White Star cider inside the phone box.

The man in the white 7.5-ton truck blows his horn at the man in the bright orange fleece jacket.

The boy of about eight in the passenger seat of a Ford Focus shouts "You fat bastard!" to the fat man at the cash machine.

The teenage boy with lots of tattoos and no shirt in late October scowls and sticks out his tongue at the little girl in the back seat of the brand new Audi.

Two young girls are in conversation. Girl on a pink Barbie bike with snot in her hair: "I'm going to my nan's and granddad's and me dad's tekkin me". Slightly older girl with bed head and pyjamas at one in the afternoon: "No you're not cos he's going scrap yard".

Two women are in conversation. Woman with dyed black crop and striped jumper: "You off up to t'church?" Slouching woman with cigarette: "Not yet." Woman with dyed black crop and striped jumper: "I thought you were off up now, I were getting stressed!"

The woman with the yellow teeth who wears her anorak indoors is shouting at her children. She doesn't get on with the man next door who sits chain-smoking in his garden all day.

Sunday, 22 November

The starlings are excitable and the flats still smell of piss. Outside, a man in jeans and a t-shirt is blowing smelly ginkgo leaves. He consolidates them into a neat pile, exposing again the small memorial stone dedicated to the dog named Mowgli and the fallen-over A-frame poster board advertising The Dana Ali Band's next appearance at the Clothiers Arms.

There's a man in a field shouting at livestock and the excitable starlings are ganging up in the nearly naked beech. Outside the big detached new-build with the statue of the bulldog by the front door, the man on the vintage motorcycle is talking to the man with Cuprinol down his top, "I'm just keeping my fingers crossed that it stays mild", he says. "I'm not so worried", says the Cuprinol man, "I've just had the van fixed and it's running like a dreeeam".

The woman in the t-shirt with 'Porn Star' written across it winces as she walks. She leans on the wall of her porch while she kicks off her muddy trainers and leaves them on the step. In the street outside, a small group of full hi-vis men are gathered around a hole in the ground. They are leaning on their tools and chatting: "He got to the middle of the field, dropped his keks, did a shit and just carried on walking…"

In the garden of the big house, there's a man in an orange helmet with a perspex visor chopping down the leylandii. At the bus stop, the old woman with the belted herringbone coat and Marks & Spencer bag-for-life is complaining about this year's I'm A Celebrity Get Me Out Of Here: "When they showed the pictures, I thought, 'I don't know any of them!'" then she adds, "It's not worth going to the hairdresser's when the weather is like this; I only went on Tuesday and it's flat as a pancake already!"

There are old women in anoraks with small grey curly dogs that match their hairdos. They are on their way to the shop that sells dusty bottles of Mateus Rosé, Lion Bars, Bisto Gravy Granules, and Andrex Toilet Tissue. The excitable starlings compete with a car alarm and the farmer who is half-in and half-out of his overalls closes his eyes as he reaches for the latch on the blind side of the gate.

Saturday, 28 November

Half-a-dozen crows, definitely crows, pick at the last remains of a dead squirrel in a squall that knocks me sideways on the bridge over the ring-road. Outside the closed down brothel, a young woman wearing only a long t-shirt and heels is in hushed discussion with a tall man in a big parka. 200 yards further along, the man with the tattooed neck stops suddenly, throws up all over the pavement, wipes his mouth on his sleeve and continues on his way. I catch his eye as I pass him. It's 3.30pm.

Earlier, the weather had been calmer. A big, feather duvet cloud was slumped over the valley head but the sky directly above was blue and still. In the leaf litter at the bottom of Mrs Brook's drive a sparrowhawk was opening up a steaming kill and, in the field behind the road sign with the buddleia growing from it, a kestrel was hovering above the half blown away barn.

Sunday, 13 December

Bin day. The low sun casts long, regular stripes of wheelie bin shadow across the road as I drive into the village. I park up and walk across the luxurious carpet of vivid green moss to Village Food & Wine: pet bedding and dried dog-food systems on display underneath a tatty awning. Inside the shop, the counter is littered with the presentation gift boxes first inspected and then dismissed by the thin, middle-aged woman in the three-quarter length anorak with the muddy hem. "No, they've all got chocolate in; she'll not eat chocolate", she says. The proprietress, a thin middle-aged woman in a torn body-warmer and jeans bends down behind the counter again, vocalising a strange involuntary exhalation as she stretches to the very back of the bottom shelf of the cabinet.

"How about this?" she says, righting herself and then setting down a plastic gift box containing a small wine glass and an even smaller bottle of pinot grigio. "What is it?" says the customer, cleaning a stripe through the greasy dust that coats it with her thumb and wiping the residue on her bulging pocket. "It's wine", explains the proprietress. "Is it dry?" "Yes, I think so." "I don't really do wine, what's it like?" "Apparently it's very nice; it's what everyone has now." "I'm not sure, I don't really do wine." "No, me neither, it makes me drunk."

The sky clouds over and the rain starts. A squall flips up the horse shit in the road, flapping it about briefly before unsticking it from the asphalt and blowing it loose down towards the old vicarage where even the stone cat that I always mistake for a swan (the tail being the neck and head) has blown over.

Back in town at the corner shop, the proprietor is sat on a stool behind the counter watching the small TV set that's balanced on top of the display of crisps. "Drug dealing," he mutters under his breath, then he looks up at me and says out loud, "Drug dealing. Is that all they've got to do in London?"

On my way home, I call at the supermarket for some milk and a packet of Mini Cheddars. Without looking up, the till woman scans my stuff and says "£1.60". As I sort through my change she stands up, leans forward and shouts down the line of checkout staff, "DOES ANYBODY NEED A WEE?" I put a £2 coin in her hand. Her colleagues all look up and shake their heads in unison. "RIGHT!" she says, "I'M GONNA BAIL OUT AFTER THIS ONE" and she nods briefly in my direction. "Thank you", I say, but she's gone.

Thursday, 14 January 2016

Stepping around the shit streaked toilet paper that trails from the drain at the

bottom of the hill, I make my way up the flotsam strewn pavement into the village: Cooper's of Stortford, Capri Sun, an empty pack-of-three Oral-B toothbrushes, a snapped off cricket bat, some Walker's salt & vinegar, a KFC box, a Cadbury's selection box, floating polystyrene, festive wrapping, an overflowing wheelie bin, half a dozen leaky black bin-liners, a bent roller-skate, and a big Porsche 4x4. The woman in the twin-set says she'd report the rubbish but she "can't do whatsit-ing," and she mimes typing on a keyboard.

There are pine needles on doorsteps.

The old man with HATE and HATE tattooed on his knuckles is complaining; his new glasses are crap and he can't see to sign his name.

The ladders slide from the roof of the Land Rover Discovery and clatter onto the road. The driver begins lashing them back into place in the heavy rain.

Mr Briggs pulls up next to the still half-flowering blue hydrangea. He winds down the window of his Suzuki Carry and points to the house opposite. He shouts above the noise of the rain and his idling engine, "They're funny buggers them; you never see 'em!" He drives away again after conceding that "He's ok, but she's a funny bugger; I've never seen her!"

The Jackdaws are cawing, and the proprietor of the shop that sells mainly marrowfat peas, salmon paste, toilet paper, and dusty bottles of Paul Masson is sitting in the dark. I open the door and he gets up from behind the counter to put the lights on.

Back outside, the small woman in the big coat at the bus stop thumbs her phone. "David Bowie's dead", she says.

Sunday, 31 January

There's a gale blowing and the tattered and bleached remains of a flag of St

George flaps furiously from the miniature manor house dovecote with the model Morris Traveller parked out front. The woman with the bin liner wrapped around the aerial of her Citroen C3 looks nervously at the straining beech trees that surround the playground, "There's that many tree-huggers in this village, we're not allowed to chop them down!" she shouts as a kestrel flies backwards over the school.

A squall rips at the surface of the flooded potholes sending miniature tsunamis flashing the full length of the street and flipping open the bonnet of the big black BMW as it rounds the corner by the church. The driver continues on his way for several seconds before stopping in the middle of the road to clamber out in his suit and pointy shoes to slam it shut again.

Eventually, the storm passes, leaving a clear blue sky dotted with glinting aircraft. The high-end plumbers' vans and the Mitsubishi pickups cast long shadows across the road; passenger seats and dashboards littered with red-top news, McDonalds bags, biros and notebooks.

On the estate, the man with the bad teeth and brown leather jacket tells me he's on the sick and bored out of his fucking mind. He says he can't really complain though because his neighbour is deaf and only has one leg.

I see a nuthatch on the bird table at the famous modernist house, a pair of yellowhammers in the long grass at the side of the farm track, and a brace of pheasants hanging from the door handle of Mr Gaunt's in the village.

Thursday, 25 February

The sun is out. Jackdaws peck at something in the road and an ambulance drifts by slowly as I follow the old woman with the done-up-to-the-top parka, pink floral leggings and four pack of Special Brew out of the newsagent's. She almost loses her balance and has to steady herself on the bin for a few seconds.

As they walk into the early sun, both the man in the lumberjack shirt and his golden retriever, are haloed by its glare. The dog stops to piss on a holly bush and the resulting cloud of vapour rises to combine with the mist of their breath, swirling around them until they almost disappear from view.

I disturb a small swarm of the first-flies-of-the-year, in the ivy by the house of the man who is wearing a football kit and no shoes.

There is orange lichen on the ridge tiles and vivid green moss on the pavements. I sidestep a young girl in wheelie-shoes and a grown-up's sweatshirt, empty arms flapping.

There's a man chopping timber in the woods with an axe: bobble hat, a pair of those reddy-brown rubberised gloves with the unbleached ribbing. And now the students are going past on the double-decker from the halls of residence that used to be the mental hospital. I was once terrified by the patients there while delivering harvest festival produce on behalf of my primary school. I remember a marrow, some tins of sweetcorn and a skinny old woman with dribble down her chin who shouted and swore and pulled at my sleeve.

The geese make that noise they make. I can still hear them all the way down at the house with the windowsill of silk flowers in Costa coffee mugs.

There's a woodpecker on the avenue of Victorian mansions. Plastic fascia boards creak in the sun. There are crocuses. People can't agree about the weather. The woman in the camel hair coat who's waiting for a taxi with three children says, "Ooh, in't it warm?", but just around the corner, the window cleaner with the woolly hat and the scarf wrapped around his face says, "By 'eck, it's cold".

There's a woman speaking in Urdu very loudly on speaker-phone at the bus stop. The other half-dozen people in the queue are finding it amusing, catching one another's eyes and laughing behind their hands.

I pass the house with the tiny cluttered garden: children's ride-on toys in faded plastic, dog shit and a fallen over grave-stone: 'Mum Gran Sadly Missed'.

The roofer with the skinny jeans and Harrington jacket says he's never had a cash card in his life, mate.

The house that was built on the field where I used to race my BMX has a poster in the window: 'SAY NO to greenfield development. SAVE OUR GREENBELT'.

Tuesday, 15 March

The recent spell of fine weather has brought other people onto the streets over which the elderly women in purple anoraks have held sole dominion in recent months.

A dozen motorcycles pass a middle-aged cyclist as he rides through the village in lycra. He rolls his eyes and shouts to me above the noise, "Hell's Angels are out!"

A middle-aged man in Crocs is chamois-ing the Skoda Yeti on the driveway of the semi-detached new-build. The sun glints off of the plastic chrome while he whistles along to 'Bad Moon Rising' on the car's stereo.

The man sitting in the driver's seat of the parked up Vauxhall Astra with the custom paint job, body kit, blacked-out windows, and 'Bang Tidy' sticker in the back, is eating a pot of Müller Rice.

Earlier, on the estate, I tried to deliver a parcel but was intercepted by a short middle-aged man with a grey side parting and a three-quarter length beige

anorak. "You can leave it with me if she's not in. She's rarely at home, she's a very active woman for a blind lady." I thanked the man and handed over the parcel. "Could you pop me a note through, just to let her know I've got it?" said the man. "I can", I said, "but how will she read it if she's blind?" The man smiled wisely, "Sense of touch", he said. Then he tapped his eye with his forefinger and explained, "When these pack up, the others pick up". "Oh", I said.

A small Asian girl with a snotty nose asks me where I'm going next. "Over that way", I say, waving my arm up the street. "Pakistan?" asks the girl.

On the track down to the house where the men from Kudos Doors (Commercial and Domestic Door Systems) are work-ing, I see a green woodpecker.

Saturday, 9 April

Stone Buddhas. Buckets of cigarette butts. Missing top stones.

The woman with the Brexit tote bag walks past the shop advertising 'Kids £4'.

Litter traps behind broken gates: energy drink cans and takeaway-styrene.

Down from where the big stuffed Tweetie Pie has been lynched from a fall pipe, a young man holding a toddler is talking to the middle-aged woman in the bathrobe. She is sipping from a pint glass.

A bag-for-life in the gutter, cat shit in the ginnel, a torn office chair and a sodden carpet in the miry garden.

Outside the house with the weed smoke wisping from the open window, a woman screams "PACK IT IN!" to the children in the back of the new Freelander.

"Fuck off! What the fuck?" shouts the man when I post his mail. The door opens and he runs across the piss soaked

carpet in the yard and up the ginnel shouting after me, "What are you fucking doing! If the dog catches you in the garden, she'll bite you, innit!" He stops next to a slimy piece of rough sawn timber and says in a more composed voice, "You need to rest it behind this bit of wood in the alleyway, innit. If the dog catches you, it's gonna bite you, innit".

Down from the witch's house with the hedge full of empty plastic bottles, I follow three men from the engineering shop on their way to the bakery. In identical overalls and of a similar build, the only thing that distinguishes them from one another is their differing stages of male pattern baldness.

The old man in the hi-vis vest is walking with both his arms outstretched, a bag-for-life full of groceries in each hand.

Two sporty young men are walking down Wood Lane, one is wearing a Nike sports bag on his back, the other, grey-marl sweatpants which he is repeatedly hoiking from his arse crack. I follow in the wake of their loud, expletive-ridden conversation and their pungent weed smoke before they turn off into the student halls of residence.

The lights are out in the shop and there's hardly any stock left, but it's still open.

Sunday, 17 April

The bin lorry is stopping every ten yards. Its loading mechanism makes a noise like that long note at the beginning of 'Rhapsody in Blue'. It dawdles its way down the long road which starts with pebble-dashed maisonettes and the smell of weed at one end and finishes with detached inter-war bungalows and the smell of seaweed fertiliser at the other. Somewhere around the middle, a man is sitting in his front room ignoring the TV while he reads Russell Grant's astrology page. Next-door, his neighbour, who is naked apart from a pair of glasses, is playing with his Playstation.

Out in the sticks, a goldfinch flies out from under my feet and the fake grass at the barn conversion is still too green to be mistaken for the real thing. I pass an open window; a woman is having an angry telephone conversation: "Well, it says here that the short length is four-and-a-half centimetres! Well, I've no idea what four-and-a-half centimetres is in inches!"

There's cherry blossom, tulips, a rusty cement mixer, leylandii, pyracantha, ruthlessly pruned buddleia, and wooden telegraph poles. A woman in one of those cream, full-length puffer coats that makes the wearer look like an enormous maggot is walking a big black greyhound.

The pub is taking bookings for New Year's Eve ('food will be served between 7–10pm'). Tonight they are serving tapas between 6-9pm and there's a wet pair of suede loafers in the hyacinth bed.

Tuesday, 17 May

I follow the minibus taxi with 'Rock'n' Roll Will Never Die' written above the back window. We pass dandelions, bluebells, flowering currant, rogue tulips, and some jackdaws pecking at a new calf.

On and up into Audi country: "Has anything changed since your last visit?" asks the dentist's receptionist. "I'm drinking much more wine", says the woman in the quilted jacket.

Outside the shop with the display of 'Worker Wagg Beef & Veg Worker Complete' dog food on the fake grass underneath the broken awning, the rain has left a long pink stripe of cherry blossom along the gutter at the edge of the road.

The sun has barely been out an hour and the men in their sixties and seventies are out too, flocking to the shop in shorts and sandals for print news.

The primary coloured lycra cyclist sets off from his garage on the new estate of concrete stone houses with plastic wooden doors. Past the pansies in pots, the developer's architectural cordyline, the not-yet-hedges of leylandii, the baby wisteria, the nursery birch and willow and the fake plastic balls of box hedge that hang from brackets next to front doors. Past the vaping Tesco delivery man. Past the Co-op delivery woman. Past the Audi, the Audi, the Audi, the Audi—and the Nissan X-Trail for when it snows. Past the builders' vans in rows seeing to the plastic doric architraves. Past the yellow millstone in the bed of polished spar. Past the blue slate chippings, the galvanised pots of lavender, the hosepipes, the solar powered garden lights and the detached garages that are too small for cars. Past For Sale boards: 'A Collection of Yorkshire's Finest Properties'. Past the Parcel Force man with the tattoo sleeves. Past the enormous blooming cherries left from when they lined the road to the old mill. And on, out into the hills.

Wednesday, 6 July

The Brexit bunting that decorates the 'No Unauthorised Vehicles' car park is tangled and twisted, the few bits of it that remain free to flap, do so with vigour. At the house opposite, the woman with the cheesecloth blouse, enormous fluffy cat shaped slippers, and the carrier bag full of soiled kitty litter is being followed down her garden path by her actual cat.

It's warm, bright and blustery and the man in his late twenties with the flat cap and florid trousers is carrying an aubergine and a tin of sardines to his BMW.

The driver of the Audi S4 throws a half-eaten pasty out of the window, almost hitting the woman who is walking past the Top Spot Snooker Club in knee length boots and a fleece jacket with wolf pictures on it.

I continue on past the sign that says 'Achieve Your Ambition Car Wash Open'. Past the lamppost with gaffer tape wrapped around it to keep the inspection cover shut. Past the soon to be closed down museum that we all visited as kids—they have a stuffed waxwing from 1970.

The wheelie bins on the new estate are the same shade of green as the fake plastic topiary in the gardens.

In the rubber scented car showroom, half-a-dozen grey haired customers in anoraks and shorts are sitting by the water cooler watching a wall-mounted television on which a grey-haired man with swollen legs is being wired up to a heart monitor on the hospital channel.

On, into the village. It's quiet apart from the blackbirds, the jackdaws and the occasional thrum of a 4x4. There are pansies, pelargoniums, 'No Cold Callers', 'Our Glorious Dead', goldfinches, martins, Sunday painters, misanthropic cows, and 'Slow Children Playing'.

Later, back in town, a man comments that I have good legs for kickboxing.

Saturday, 23 July

30°C

The ragwort in the back of Mr Brooke's Transit pick-up is a couple of feet tall now and the dead badger in the road isn't a dead badger, it's a Ramones t-shirt.

The fishmonger drops the pan from his scales onto the floor with a loud clang, "Throwing the tackle around!" he says as he bends to pick it up. The postman walks in and drops a bundle of mail onto the counter, "Don't you get fed up of delivering rubbish?" the fishmonger asks.

On the housing estate on the moor where juvenile starlings intermingle with pheasants, the smell of warm porches is oddly comforting. There are fake lawns, stone turtles, small colourful plastic huskies and a skip with broken drones in it.

At the high altitude newsagent's shop, the proprietor says he doesn't get away much. The last holiday he had was a long weekend to Amsterdam. He says he didn't really enjoy it because the lads he went with ate too much 'cake' and spent the whole time asleep.

At the big house in the shadow of the wind turbine, a man in a country check shirt, khaki shorts, deck shoes and white socks is reading print news and sipping Pimm's under an awning. Two care workers arrive in an old black Fiesta, unhitch the gate and make their way into the back garden trailing bin liners.

On the council estate of men in shorts and women in anoraks, there are cherries on the pavement and wood pigeons flapping in the leylandii. Two men in their seventies are talking across a privet: "It's like when Muhammad Ali came over here and fought Brian London, the Blackpool Rock…"

A ten-year-old people carrier loaded up with bulk bought dog-food-systems pulls up outside the flats with the rusty grab handles by the front doors.

Grandparents and grandchildren play swing-ball and the ice cream van plays 'Oranges and Lemons'.

Two teenage boys in an old Vauxhall Corsa—windows down, no shirts—are blowing their car horn in time to the music on the radio and the man in the striped apron who is tending his vegetable garden mutters "Dickheads!" under his breath.

The dock leaves are getting big, daisies are coming through, hydrangeas are starting to flower. There is clover in the grass and there are sunbaked slugs on the sticky asphalt.

On the brand new estate of reconstituted stone semis and developer planted lavender, bald men in their sixties and seventies wear shorts and shades to walk their tousled grey hairpiece terriers.

At the caravan showroom where everything is black and white, black or white coffee is on draft. Black and white flags flutter in the paddock and black and white staff lean on things authoritatively. A large tattooed man in union-jack shorts and mirror shades is checking out the Bailey Pageant Bretagne while a man in khaki shorts, a striped canvas belt and an Oxford shirt is examining the Hymer Exsis which is parked up by the striking yellow daisy bushes. A slim, tanned man in his early thirties, with big 1980s hair, earrings, tight short shorts, espadrilles and a black and white body-hugging shirt with 'WANG' written across the back, makes his way between the plastic tub of thirsty pansies and the run-over florets of broccoli into the shop. He strikes up a conversation with the shop manager in an unusually deep voice "…all right, mate. I'll see you later then, pal".

Monday, 15 August

6:30am: Light drizzle. The man in the pink t-shirt and distressed denim jeans blows his nose noisily while the jogger who is circumnavigating the pond in the park scatters frightened ducklings from their roost under the overhang of the edging stones.

Mr Bateman has a new number 9 on his front door. Unusually, he has decided not to remove the old brass one and has opted instead to fasten a new, slightly smaller (brass effect) plastic one directly over the top of it. From a distance, the resulting collage is completely illegible.

The individual barcode stickers on each of the stone setts laid at the barn conversion a couple of years ago have finally worn away leaving dark rectangular stains where they once were.

The concierge with the Polyveldt shoes and black polo shirt says he hasn't had a pay rise in nine years. "I'm going to jack it in and have a couple of months in Goa", he says. "Champion!" exclaims the man in the grey flannels and Oxford shirt from deep inside his rose garden.

I round a corner into the back alley of the terrace. Two tanned men are kissing on a doorstep. On seeing me, the older of them says, "I'm his grandad, by the way" and the younger man—gold earrings and dressing gown—doubles over, laughing. "We're not that way inclined", reiterates the older man, irritated, "and if you are, then I sympathise!"

A few doors down, an angry woman in a sari brandishes a yard brush at her neighbour: "Keep your fucking children under fucking control!" she screams, "Fucking leave me a-fucking-lone!" A black cat wearing a cobweb cowl watches on from behind the wheelie bins.

The weeds between the flags on the narrow pavements are knee high in some of the back streets—mainly long grasses and ragwort. I graze my knuckles on a concrete lamp post on the narrow pavement as I squeeze past the man with the slicked back nicotine hair. He falls backwards into a hedge but rebounds upright again to continue on his way.

The spectral flâneur who wears all-year-round head-to-toe waterproofs comes out of the bottom of Grasmere Road, turns left towards the park, then turns around and runs back again. It's the first time I've seen him since March 23rd, 2012.

Later, at the shattered old farm on the moor, the middle-aged Flora Poste who has moved in at one of the cottages is tending her hanging baskets. Since she arrived a few months ago, the decrepit doors and aching window frames have been painted a fashionable eau de nil

and there are crushed cloves in the yard. Her influence has yet to reach the main house where there is still dog sick on the doorstep and a badly written note in the porch window: 'Leave parcels In the WOODSHED'.

Sunday, 28 August

A gale sluices the first fallen leaves along the gutter and the man with the screwed up face who is jogging into the wind barely overtakes me. Brake lights cast the gates of the park red and a cyclist pulls over to adjust his gaiters.

In town, the rough sleeping couple have moved from their usual pitch in the doorway of the pawnbrokers to the more sheltered entrance of the strip club.

In the suburbs, a woodpigeon perches on top of the new LED street light and the tired chubby woman at the show home says "Hello" with long, roadkill flat vowels, rising and falling in inflection either side of the 'L'.

I say good morning to the man with the silver earrings, unzipped gilet, grey goatee and rat-tail but he doesn't reply.

I struggle to read the dull screen of my PDA and the security man at the factory gates asks me whether it was made in China. "I've no idea", I say. "Nothing they make works. They're rubbish!" I point out that most of the manufacturing at his factory has famously been transferred to China over the last ten years. He looks sheepish, thinks for a moment and then says, "All I'm saying is I've got a 1963 Massey Ferguson tractor and It still goes like new and it's British made".

On the TV monitor in the pro shop at the golf club, a muscular American man with American hair and American teeth is playing golf in the sunshine with palm trees behind him and a heavy rock guitar soundtrack. He looks up at the camera to say he can't believe how comfortable his trousers are. Meanwhile, the door to the shop opens and a short fat bald man with a grey moustache rustles in wearing a waterproof jacket and ill-judged shorts. He takes off the jacket, hangs it over the telly and wipes the rain off his glasses with a handkerchief.

It's 11.30am and the smell of stewing meat pervades the estate of retired 1970s Britain. The narrow paths are cluttered with architectural features in UPVC. There are gates to open every couple of yards and redundant miniature porches that I have to walk backwards out of because there's no room to turn around. There are unnecessary steps leading to raised beds of marigolds, box topiary, begonia, and there are swathes of hard-standing devoted solely to the display of miniature plastic fauna.

Two men are talking in the street. One wears his Hawaiian shirt untucked with the top two buttons undone, the other has Brylcreem hair, heavy black plastic-rimmed glasses, and a purple nylon shirt tucked into grey polyester slacks. They are discussing their experiences of electrocardiography: "It makes your arm twitch, doesn't it?" Inside the house, a woman in a dinner-lady tabard sits watching *Bargain Hunt* with her right hand clasped idly around the handle of a vacuum cleaner.

Swallows gather eagerly on phone lines.

Tuesday, 11 October

Greenhead Park, 6.30am: The glowing disembodied head of the man staring into his phone floats towards me in the dark. We pass each other and I recognise him as the early adopter hipster man who shaved off his beard and twirly moustache about five years ago.

Out in the sticks, 11am: The wind rushes through trees with a dry autumn hiss, each gust followed by a shower of beech nuts onto asphalt or a clatter of acorns onto car bonnets. There's fruit from a cherry laurel too, and birch seeds, and

conkers, and moulted feathers all littering the pavement.

The brand new Stanley safety boot that appeared on the doorstep of number 9 on Monday morning has today migrated up the road to number 3 via number 7 yesterday.

The man in the old anorak at the house on the moor is going to Cape Verde for a couple of weeks. He says he's sick of this country because it's too depressing. All the gold that he painted his mailbox with in honour of the Olympic Games four years ago has worn off and it's back to its old rusty red.

On past the dangerously weathered drystone wall and the big handwritten sign on the garage door: 'GOT you / ON CAMERA / BASTARDS / ALL VALUBLES / GONE TO SAFETY / SO / piss OFF / XXXXX / SHoT GUN / BEHIND DOOR'.

In the yard of the old farmhouse, next to the magpie cage traps, a cat and three kittens are eating a dead rabbit.

There are wasps in the ivy at the house of the woman with the plasters on her forehead.

Back in town at the 1970s Beauty Board offices, there are black briefcases for the boys and gaily coloured desk tidies for the girls. A flat backed woman in a cardigan with tissues up her sleeve shuffles about saying "Thanks, love", and the man with the rolled up sleeves writes on the spine of a box file in marker pen; he stands the file on a shelf next to half-a-dozen others and has a quick sniff of the pen nib before replacing the lid.

On the aspirational estate of barely detached new builds where nobody is ever at home, there are pansies in the borders and cans of Car Plan Tyre Silk on the doorsteps. I set off a chain of barking guard dogs: as one jumps down from a lounge window as I pass, so another at the house next door jumps up, upsetting the potted orchids in miniature galvanised buckets and the resin statues of kissing lovers whose entwined bodies make the shape of a love heart.

Sunday, 6 November

There's a chill in the air. There are starlings. There is standing traffic because a bus has got stuck. The driver is wearing sunglasses and waving his arms at a woman in a Fiesta—who is also stuck. There's a navy blue sock in the gutter.

I walk past the dog-eared 'Vote Remain' posters in the window of the railway bookshop and take the desire line across the verge. The yellow carpet of fallen leaves under the now thin canopy of the cherry tree is accented with black: seven empty White Star cider cans and a plastic bag of dog shit.

I cross the road. The clothing bank is propped up on bricks, there's a new chipboard fence and the kerbstones have been messily daubed with white paint: 'No Parking Please'.

Schoolgirls are stealing schoolboys' hats for fun and the man who jogs in his suit trousers overtakes me in the road, his grey shirt completely buttoned—including the cuffs.

I slalom around on wheelie bin pavements. At number 56, the bin has a brass effect '5' and '6' bolted to it, next door the '58' has been applied with lackadaisical Tippex and outside number 60 there's no wheelie bin at all, just a small five-litre brushed steel pedal bin with no number.

A single rubberised red-brown glove with off-white cuffing lies in the gutter. This is by far the most commonly discarded style of glove in the Huddersfield area.* I once saw one fall from the back of a builder's truck as it rounded a corner which perhaps explains the phenomenon.
(*Huddersfield Glovewatch 2002)

Further up the hill, the soot-black terraces give way to pebble-dash inter-war semis with neatly trimmed privet. There's a pile of interior doors in a ginnel and a big ball of hoover fluff on a lawn but no more White Star cans.

A strong easterly breeze is blowing now and the leaves on the pavement are getting deep. There are parked cars on the right, ivy encroaching from the left and overhanging trees above.

Higher up again and the uniformity of another Victorian terrace is broken with a UPVC porch, a satellite TV dish, or a clump of Pampas grass. Opposite this, behind the collapsed dry stone wall there's an area of literal edgeland: rough tussock grass, arthritic nettles, fireweed, brambles, a broken pallet, a graffiti-daubed electricity substation, the remains of a galvanised security palisade and a sheer millstone drop to the valley bottom.

Tuesday, 15 November

5.40am: It's raining steadily and the reflection of the traffic lights in the road surface reaches the full hundred yards to my feet. Mostly all I can hear is the rustle of waterproofs, the rain on my hood and the burble of the run-off channel in the gutter. Occasionally a car tears past in a belligerent hiss of spray.

Later, on the estate of sixties-built semis, the solar panels on the new lampposts are covered with an inch-and-a-half of settled snow and the starlings are whistling in the tops of the yellow trees. The roofer says he's going to finish work early so he can go and buy his girlfriend a watch for a hundred pounds and the woman in the leggings and military parka says her fox terrier is much better in hisself, thank you.

Leonard Cohen has died and the junction box by the flats has started to hum loudly.

The sun comes out lighting up the green baize pavements and I knock off my hat

on an inconspicuous washing line for the second time. Rows of plastic clothes pegs in faded primaries highlight the next three low-slung lines and I avoid these by bowing gracefully like Kate Middleton in the 1902 State Landau.

At the entrance to the flats, two men in their fifties are engaged in a loud debate about Lorne sausage. "It shouldn't be called sausage at all because it's square and sausages are round. It's more like a square burger", insists the one with the bit of arse crack showing. The one without the bit of arse crack showing counters, "If it's sausage meat, it's sausage. End. Of."

Donald Trump is president-elect of the U.S.A.

On the estate where the old ladies in purple anoraks still call me "Love", the air is thick with the fug of Stardrops, stewing steak and cheap tobacco. Everyone gathers to inspect the last sweet pea flowers of the year.

I pass the boy who once tried to sell me a pebble for a pound. He's too old for that stuff now.

I call in at the newsagent's for some crisps but the shelves are completely bare apart from a few tabloid news-papers. The proprietor sits behind the till wearing a scarf and hat.

A taxi pulls up outside the house whose steps are littered with sodden Capri Sun cartons, nail polish bottles, chocolate coins, smashed crockery, a baby monitor, sherbet straws, empty portion control packs of tomato ketchup, a pair of nail scissors, and a bent and twisted purple glittery stars-on-a-spring ornament—like a deely-bopper for your windowsill. The taxi driver blows his horn to notify the occupants of his arrival but the driver of an oncoming Fiesta thinks it's directed at him and gestures aggressively, contorting his face in unadulterated rage.

Fat flies gather on white UPVC to garner the last vestige of residual heat.

Wednesday, 7 December

5.30am: It's windy and fallen leaves are following me down the street. The man who wears head-to-toe waterproofs whatever the weather is twenty yards in front of me on the other side of the road. He makes to cross over to my side but when he sees me he dithers briefly and turns back. He then runs the hundred yards to the traffic lights at the bottom and turns right into town.

I slip in a patch of rock salt on Victoria Street where Alan Titchmarsh's noughties decking is slimy and rotten and the woman with the NHS lanyard is smoking on her doorstep.

Margaret is in the bistro with her coat on eating fried eggs, chips, beans, and milky tea.

The woman at the bus stop says that the sport of boxing is "a work of art".

Out in the sticks, it starts to rain heavily and the last of the autumn leaves line the gutters yellow. At one of the big houses on the ridge, I can see two photographs through the glass front door: an informal group shot of men wearing chinos, and the front end of a 1980s Porsche 924 taken from a low angle.

At the manor house golf club, the food smells like 1970s school dinners and the sign in the car park says 'Residence Parking'. There's a dead shrew on the drive under the enormous poplars.

Up in the village, there's a Jaguar parked on every other street corner and the air is fresh apart from the occasional whiff of a wood-burning stove.

Beech hedges rustle their parchment leaves in the wind and the starlings are swanee whistling in the tops of the trees. I stop to talk to the man who is building the septic tank. He tells me he used to be a line engineer for the National Grid. I ask him how they get the cables across ravines and valleys and he says they usually use fishing line and a bow and arrow but on one occasion he used a model aeroplane.

Four mud-spattered men with half-a-dozen spaniels pass us, they are followed by a quad bike with three dozen dead pheasants slung over a line across the back.

Back in town, the old man in the beige anorak and matching polyester slacks with frayed hems has taken exception to the music coming from the Skoda Octavia Estate. "Turn your music down!" he growls aggressively. The Skoda man blows cigarette smoke out of the window and ignores him and the old man skulks away with his heavy bags for life (one from the Co-op and one from Sainsbury's).

Friday, 13 January 2017

It's dark in the park because they've turned out the lights to save some money. There's a noisy owl in the wooded bit and the man with the little round glasses says he's fucking freezing.

It's 1° and the frost is still hard when I pass the man in the t-shirt, shorts and flip-flops who is struggling to fit a baby seat into an old Ford Focus. Across the street a thin woman is forcing cardboard packaging into her overflowing bin, "Fuck me!" she says to the teenage girls who are listening to speaker-phone hip-hop on the wall, "When are they gonna come and empty the chuffin' bins, man?"

Down by the 'No Fly Tipping' sign someone has fly tipped a broken wheelie bin.

At the bottom of the hill between the two derelict fridges, two boys of about eight or nine are playing kerby while another boy throws small stones at them. They pause briefly when the angry old man in the polyester parka poises a

tin can across the street. He climbs into a black Skoda Fabia and drives away at high speed and the boys carry on with their game.

Next to the end terrace with 'NOTE PRIVT PlS DON'T THROW RUBISH HERE' painted on its gable end in foot high lettering there are three sodden old settees, two armchairs, a stained king-sized mattress, a wardrobe door, four split open bin liners of children's clothing in a puddle, a small pile of rubble, a large cardboard box, a bit of an old tent, an empty Pepsi can, an empty Persil box and some snapped off bits of rotten timber.

On the side street of semis, a tall thin man in a black fleece and beanie is trying to look nonchalant while his dog pisses on his next door neighbour's gate post. He glances casually through the front window to check he hasn't been spotted. On the other side of the road, outside the house with the plastic-terracotta doorstep plant pots of couch grass and Haribo wrappers, the woman in her sixties is being patient with her Yorkshire terrier as it shits on the pavement. She stands over it anxiously with a little black plastic bag ready in her hand. Further along, there's a pride of journalists with woollen overcoats and long lenses blocking the road outside the house of the man who was shot dead by the police yesterday.

Back in town, the Sports Direct assistant idly plays with his genitals while he waits for the young girl to try on some trainers.

Saturday, 28 January

A scrappy formation of 258 geese honk in the sky above topiary conifers and slimy green millstone.

At the building site, the foreman with the obvious wig says, "Ooh, my condoms have arrived" as he takes the large parcel from me. He looks around the Portakabin for the approval of his hi-vis colleagues but they are all too busy eating their Pot Noodles. I smile politely and leave, kicking a small hamster of sphagnum down the wooden steps in front of me.

Fieldfares flock in the field behind the cottage with the fake shutters that aren't big enough for the windows.

Leylandii hide the double-parked cars and block the winter sun. It's warm. There are midges. The birds think it's spring: woodpigeons, sparrows, starlings, a woodpecker, and the big flock of gulls circling above the tree line.

The moors are invisible in the mist and the men in their sixties at the clubhouse stand in groups of grey and navy with their hands in pockets, rocking on their heels. Their conversations about whether Chris or Darren should "look after the technical side when Geoff's gone" are punctuated with the bleeping of Audi key fobs.

At the new-build fake-sandstone semis where the people carriers have 'Centre Parcs' stickers on their windscreens and the gardens are still littered with firework casings, the builders are loading a heavy-duty radio into a van, "Get yourself home, get your lunch and get your leg over and I'll meet you back here this aft'"

'Never Mind The Dog, Beware Of The Owner.'

Wednesday, 15 February

Past the beech tree with the polystyrene takeaway tray in its lower branches and the bin liner flapping from its bare canopy.

Past the primary colours of the nursery school: "Be careful of Mia's knee please Brandon".

Past the prefab school of dance and the rotten green Scout hut.

Past the woman in black tassels who is standing still in the middle of the road, distracted by her phone.

Past the big cardboard box, squashed and wedged between the lamppost and the wall.

Past dead twigs in plastic pots, bent railings, leaded lights repaired with packing tape, the closed down pub with the dirty windows…

Left, down the cobbles and moss. Bare trees overhang green stone walls outside the 1980s vicarage where a blackbird is sounding the alarm and two stocky terriers are fighting by the overgrown chainlink tennis court.

Dog owners shout.

The fake bells of All Saints ring out from the PA in the church tower and the fat man in the Octavia empties his ashtray into the gutter.

There's a man mending a caravan and shouting for Susan.

The rag-and-bone man drives past the flats at high speed and rattles right by the house with the decorative concrete wall while the woman (maybe Susan?) in tight jeans and purple fleece looks on disapprovingly.

The smell of the Aussie Burger grill is on the breeze outside Taste Buds takeaway—Is it the Aussie Burgers or is it weed? Maybe a bit of both.

Drink cans and takeaway packaging have been impaled on the wrought iron railings around the basketball court and down behind the broken old concrete fence where there's a big view across the valley, the man in the noisy JCB is 'Improving Yorkshire's Sewers'.

At the bottom of the narrow stone steps, the tall thin man with the dew drop on his nose stands on a portion control sachet of ketchup and it sticks to his shoe. I say "Good morning" as we pass and he ignores me. At the top

of the steps, his discarded tab end is still burning out next to a big flob of gob.

Wednesday, 1 March

Police sirens and heavy sleet.

I follow the drunk man with the old Sainsbury's bag-for-life who is making use of the full width of the generous pavements. He wears a three-quarter length camouflage jacket, skinny jeans, and an enormous pair of brothel creepers. He goes into the Co-op at the second attempt and buys a bag of salmon and potato dog food.

Down from the dumpster of brand new trainers, at the terrarium bus stop where ivy thrives behind the perspex, the women with the toddlers in pushchairs are discussing a mutual neighbour: "That twat over the road".

A series of tiny swastikas have been etched into the pink CND graffiti on the junction box at the corner of the street. Next to it, a skinny man in a hooded top and tracksuit is gesticulating angrily to me as I perform a three-point-turn in the road. I wind down my window, "What?" I shout, exasperated. "You could have fucking done that in one!" says the hoody man, grinning. I smile, "Only if I'd gone onto the verge, I didn't want to damage the grass." "Fuck the grass!" says the hoody man. I laugh and the hoody man waves as I drive away.

It starts to snow and I pass a man riding a self-balancing board down the other side of the road. He's pushing a baby in a pushchair past the bathroom scales that have been left propped against the base of a lamppost.

The snow gets heavier and an old Renault Mégane pulls onto a driveway. Quite a large woman gets out wearing fluffy slippers and a silk dressing gown with a dragon motif embroidered onto

the back. She walks quickly to the house as large snowflakes settle on top of her luxuriant mahogany perm.

I make my way up the path to the house where Smokie's greatest hit blasts from an open window. A man in his sixties answers the door: unshaven, bare feet, casual jogging pants. "I'm surprised to see you today", he says, "I didn't realise you delivered on Sundays". "I don't", I say, "It's Monday". "Shit! Is it?" exclaims the man, "What time is it?"

Two women in matching purple anoraks (the one on the left also has purple hair) are out for a brisk stroll in the woods. The sun has come out highlighting the tyre tracks on Mucky Lane. Holly trees glisten and squirrels scramble among the snowdrops. The clouds clear and the wet road surface that winds through the glade of expensive detached new-builds becomes a mirror reflecting retro' oriel windows, fake lead flashings and jaunty medieval-lite gables. "It's like a magical wonderland", says the woman without the purple hair.

A van passes. Written on its side in a neat sans-serif it says 'Making Tomorrow a Better Place'.

Sunday, 19 March

"I was thinking lily but that's not a flower, is it?" says the drunk woman at 6am.

The wind assists me up the hill and blows the blossom from the trees outside the house where a five-litre plastic container of screen-wash has been placed in each corner of the small front garden.

I turn down the poorly maintained track with the big view across the valley and pass the wheelie bins of the terrace with more greenery in the guttering than in the paved over gardens.

There are primulas on the verges under polythene trees where a flock of noisy goldfinches has been squabbling all week.

I follow a black and white cat onto the estate of headless Buddhas, tailless schnauzers, earless rabbits, faded anoraks and unfashionable bell-bottom jeans in indigo. A grey-haired man in chinos places a four pack of Galahad Premium Lager and a bag of green potatoes on his neighbour's doorstep next to the faded plastic meerkats on a seesaw.

Along the valley side past the discarded *Top Bottoms* DVD and the junction box graffiti. Past the Muslim man, trousers tucked into socks. Past the teenage boys in tracksuits tops who are sharing a joint. It's sunny now, 19°, but the woman with the tasselled gold scarf is still hiding under the hood of her heavy coat.

The police helicopter hovers overhead as two women at the bus stop discuss the sexual assault featured in the local paper. "You can't risk anything now, can you?" the younger woman says, "I was thinking of walking into work now the weather's getting better but I'm not risking it". "I usually walk in", says the older woman, "If they see me they'll run a mile anyway".

Mouldy windfall apples line the slippery stone steps to the back-to-backs. I walk head first into the hanging basket of dead twigs next to the front door with 'fucking crack bitch' scrawled across it in marker pen. I curse and make my way back out to the Co-op where I sit in the car park eating peanuts while the man with the Father Christmas bag-for-life hugs a spaniel.

Friday, 14 April

6am, overcast, light rain.

In the park, the man smoking strong weed is walking his Akita past the temperance fountain. There are the joggers, ornamental lampposts, the shut up ice-cream pergola, the Boer war soldier, and on the steep hill, there's the modern-day Sisyphus struggling with his 10kg bag of potatoes; every day I pass him here.

Further down, another young man is threatening to jump from the railway bridge on Church Street. The police are turning back the traffic and a woman is shouting.

Lunchtime now, and the jackdaws are pecking at the horse shit in Wakefield Road while a group of old men gather around the modular seating at the Hyundai showroom that smells of rubber.

Clouds clear, it's 15° and big flies are basking on the white front doors of the terrace. I pass a man in canvas espadrilles and a wide-brimmed straw hat down by the junction box with its doors open and wiring exposed. He's talking to the young Sikh man who is sitting in his expensive black Mercedes with the roof down and his sunglasses on.

The council are mowing the lawn under the Pampas grass on Lawton Street and, on the new estate, the developer-planted cherry and viburnum are finally usurping the fake plastic topiary.

"…Betty, its telling me you've put the wrong pin number in, love. Will you take it out and try again? No, no, wait for me, Betty. That's it. Okay, you can put your pin in now, Betty"

A heron flies the length of Fenay Bridge Road and the woman in the three-quarter length taupe anorak is imperious. She stares Britannia like into the distance as her terrier pisses on the cotoneaster next to the Vauxhall Vectra with the bulldog bumper sticker.

A chunky young man with a regulation hairstyle and a Burberry check coat walks with his head on one side into the Food & Wine shop. He noticeably grimaces as he picks up two cans of Skol Super. "Two pounds please, love", says the avuncular woman in the turtleneck behind the counter.

In the 1970s village populated by the grown-up cast of a Children's Film Foundation movie and *Stig of the Dump*, most people in the bungaloid extensions share surnames with kids I went to primary school with. The daffodils are out in the churchyard and the jackdaws are squabbling violently as a Radiophonic Workshop soundtrack plays in my head.

At the Frank Lloyd-Lite gated community on the hill where the dog walkers drive Mercedes vans, the cottage gardens are being torn up and replaced with 'Driveways of Distinction' by young men who listen to hip-hop on site radios.

Sunday, 21 May

"Oh, I didn't know he'd ordered a jockey wheel", says the woman with bleached hair and red shorts. "DEAN, YOUR JOCKEY WHEEL'S ARRIVED!"

There's a long cerise pink hairpiece on the stone steps up to Pip Hill from Albert Street.

At the house with the laughing terracotta Buddha on the broken patio, there's a plastic Christmas wreath and a dozy looking vine weevil on the front door. The plants in the pots are all dead and two women in their twenties are sitting on the doorstep in their pyjamas, smoking. A black Mercedes Smart car is parked on the drive, its boot decorated with a big iron cross motif and the word 'Luftwaffe' in a gothic font.

It's mild and overcast and the pervading smell is of liver and onions. At the house with the grinning miniature Easter Island heads, I say hello to the man who is posting flyers for the local curry house into the letterbox that says 'No Junk Mail'. He doesn't reply.

Next door, a three-foot-high pile of rubbish has accumulated in the garden and there are now fourteen sycamore saplings growing from between the joints in the cracked concrete paving flags. On the drive, the old Vauxhall Vectra has six nodding bulldogs wearing cross of St George t-shirts arranged across its parcel shelf.

The bin men ignore the bright yellow toilet with the wooden lid that's been left out with the wheelie bin.

The thin man who is driving the car transporter for the insurance company likes to be known as 'J-Dog' according to the shiny cut-out tin foil writing in the window of his cab.

The man in the pastel coloured shirt at the Co-op is buying himself a Costa coffee. "I only need five hours sleep a night", he says to the woman behind the counter, "If I don't get it though, I'm as sick as a dog!" "I'm the same!" says the woman. "I just know when I'm overtired and I just have to go to bed." "So you should", says the man, "Nothing wrong with that! You're like me".

There's a thrush singing in the top of a leylandii.

A big forty-odd-year-old man with a homemade face tattoo pulls up on a child's glittery pink push bike with a flat tyre and asks me, "Have you fucking been up fucking New Laithe with a fucking parcel?"

Five minutes later, an old Ford Focus skids around the corner. Three of the doors open before it even stops and half-a-dozen big men jump out, smash the front windows of a VW Golf and drag out the driver.

Wednesday, 21 June

It's raining, a strong breeze is swinging the phone cables and occasional gusts blow litter past me in the road. I walk up the hill behind the man with the Viking hair and beard who is wearing pyjamas and slippers.

In the park, the big man in his twenties with analeptic leg shakes and an eagle print t-shirt is sitting on a bench smoking weed. He's listening to some reggae-influenced pop music on speaker-phone and his attempts to sing along elicit only occasional growls and shouts of elongated hybrid vowels.

Outside the care home, the couch grass between the flags of the pavement has dried yellow since the council treated it at the beginning of the week. in the car park, staff in waterproofs sit on kerb-stones smoking cigarettes and drinking mugs of tea.

I pass the garden where hundreds of small succulents are displayed. They are housed in dozens of planters made from rough slices of birch attached to the rails of the perimeter fence with expanding foam.

The big forty-odd-year-old man with the homemade face tattoo appears on his little girl's bike again. I wonder whether he's trying to intimidate me when he starts pulling shit wheelies in the road and grunting like a wild animal. He has a big gold chain around his neck and most of his arse crack is showing.

Starlings squawk from the guttering.

Later, on the semi-detached suburban estate where people wear Crocs to chamois their Skoda Yetis, the plastic topiary has bleached in the sun leaving it a psychedelic turquoise against the acid green of the fake lawns.

On the edge of the estate, the new owners of the farmhouse have replaced the broken Land Rover Defender and the piles of cow shit on the drive with a brace of high-performance German saloons and a statue of the Buddha.

Windowsill survey: a scented candle, a small porcelain model of a flower barrow, a porcelain goose and gosling, a ceramic lighthouse, a hedgehog ornament made from a pine cone, a basket of colourful

silk roses, a small clay model of a terrace of houses, an ornamental statuette of a couple kissing, their intertwined bodies making the shape of a love heart, a scented candle inside a small birdcage, a piece of MDF painted white with the word 'Love' cut out of it, a vase of daffodils, a dead pelargonium, an empty jam jar, two silk gerberas in a milk bottle, two Christmas cacti, two brass effect resin rabbit ornaments, an ornamental teapot and kettle, more silk gerberas, a kind of imitation Fabergé egg on a gold effect stand, a white porcelain dolphin, a pair of ornamental statuettes of topless women holding tea lights, a glass vase filled with colourful glass beads and two silk more gerberas, a book leant against the window displaying the cover: We May Not Have It All Together But Together We Have It All, a boxer dog (a real one).

Monday, 3 July

Out in the sticks a tiny vole dives for cover in the wall of the converted barn and maniacal starlings yell incoherently from the guttering. The builders' site radio blasts 'I Don't Like Mondays' by The Boomtown Rats around the new estate. It is, of course, Monday, and it's very warm.

A large moth is caught mid-flight by a pied wagtail who smashes it against the asphalt of the Rooneys' driveway. The moth escapes briefly but is chased down again, stamped on and repeatedly pecked at. Again it limps free, half flying and half bouncing across the Rooneys' lawn. The wagtail moves in a third time and the moth is finally dispatched. It's a big meal and the bird struggles to swallow it before flittering off somewhere amongst the Rooneys' statues of racoons pushing wheelbarrows and playing guitars.

Mr Brown has moved from the big house to one of the cottages a few doors down. The delivery man asks the woman in the bucket hat who is bent over weeding the verge of the pretty lane, "Has Mr Brown moved to this one?" "Yes", says the woman. "I wasn't sure." "It's definitely that one", says the woman waving her trowel at the Range Rover on the drive, "I was over there this morning and I saw his vegetables".

A bullfinch circles my head, I duck and the woman with the thick plastic rimmed glasses in the big picture window laughs at me over the top of her computer monitor.

Addy's Picnic Hamper van signals its arrival at the cardboard box factory gates with loud 'Greensleeves' chimes. A forklift driver abandons his truck and runs across the yard to be the first in the queue. Seconds later there's a squeaking of doors and about a dozen men in overalls file out reaching into pockets and sorting change.

I knock at the door of the old manor house. "Come in ladies!" says a voice from inside. I open the door a crack and shout, "It's the postman!" "Come on in girls!" says the voice again "It's the postman!" I shout again. "Ooo, soup for lunch, how lovely!" says the voice. "It's the postman", I say walking in with the mail. "Oh look, it's the postman", says the smart old man in the damask armchair.

At the house on the ridge of the valley side, the man with the wire-rimmed glasses, grey sweatshirt, and jeans is making use of the pejorative overtones of the word 'titivate' while describing his neighbour's new LED outdoor lighting display.

Back in town, the thin woman with one leg of her grey tracksuit tucked into a turquoise sock asks whether I'm a postman. I say I am. "I love postmen", she says. "That's great", I say "Yeah, they always take my letters to Portugal", she explains.

A thin man in filthy baggy jeans and enormous dirty white trainers walks down Newsome Road with his head in his hands. He must be able to see through a crack in his fingers because he keeps going like this for about fifty yards.

At the post office, an elderly woman is holding up the queue while she explains to the cashier at length her frustration at having been held up in the queue.

Tuesday, 1 August

Walking into work at 6am, I am overtaken by a man on an old mountain bike, a Labrador on a lead trotting alongside him. Twenty yards ahead of me, on the pavement, is the spectral flâneur who I've occasionally glimpsed sight of over many years as he conducts his fast-paced early morning dérives around town. He is easily recognised by his head-to-toe navy blue waterproofs and tightly drawn hood—whatever the weather. Over time I have imbued this man with supernatural powers of perception and am consequently intimidated by his presence in the same street as me. Eventually, the mountain biker and Labrador catch up with and then pass the mysterious flâneur which appears to prompt him to take flight and he sprints across the road, disappearing into a side street for another few months.

I have a badly addressed parcel to deliver; no street number, just a name. I ask the camp eastern European man with the tattoos who lives at the house with the waist height grass meadow in the front yard whether he recognises it. He says he doesn't which seems to frustrate him. I can tell he really wants to help and, after thinking for a moment he says, "The only advice I can give you is to drive really slowly along the road looking in all the windows at the curtains and things".

It's windy. I can hear plastic bottles blowing down the street. I see one bounce past the little junction box whose inspection door has been secured shut with brown packing tape.

Balls of plastic topiary hang from chains by front doors on the new estate. There are low maintenance bits of lawn, bits of privet, bits of cotoneaster etc. On a window sill, a pair of metallic effect picture frames display identical pieces of white paper printed with the words '4x4 Metallic Effect Frame'.

At the house that smells of dog piss, there are signs on the gate that say 'Beware of Dogs'. Next door, at the house where a recording of an Islamic call to prayer is audible from an upstairs window, there is a handwritten note in pencil stuck to the door frame above the doorbell that says 'What are YOU saying?'

The sun comes out briefly and broken glass glistens on the pavements. A scattering of white takeaway detritus blows in a circle outside the post office where the couple with the bags for life are having an argument at the bus stop.

Inside the newsagent's shop with the faded sign, a big man on crutches is talking to the thin woman in the torn gilet behind the counter. He is dressed all in black with his hood up. He says Dr Who has had too many assistants over the years. "It started with his granddaughter and she was around for a while and then a new one came in and she'd be gone before you knew it and then there'd be another female on" he explains, "There have been that many assistants it's hard to keep up sometimes".

On the estate of sweet peas and sticky grass, the 4x4 is all loaded up on the driveway and the kids strapped in for the holiday drive. Parents scurry back and forth, "Have you got your fidget spinners?"

"Well, she's putting enough weight on for twins", says the waitress at the pub as she walks past the bar with plates of serviettes and ketchup stacked the length of her forearm. The barman glances up from his phone with a wry smile.

I pass The Bathstore on the ring road and I find myself thinking about the olive green bath panel that was on sale for years at the rural post office from where I used to collect the mail. Other than post office essentials: stamps, envelopes, pens etc. there was nothing else for sale but this olive green bath panel. It was hung from baling twine above the cashier's head and had a price tag of eighteen pounds attached to it. The office is long since gone and presumably the bath panel will have gone with it.

Saturday, 26 August

Leaves are stuck fast to the roofs of cars with condensation. More leaves and a couple of energy drink cans line the gutter. I can hear a police siren, the noise of a train going through the cutting, a jangle of keys as a man unlocks the community centre. There's a woodpigeon calling from the beech on the edge of the wood. There are some more old mattresses in the front garden of the flats and a burst bin bag outside A-Z Tyres where the fuchsia had dropped its flowers in a neat purple stripe. In the park, a flock of gulls swoops over the narrow gauge railway and the Canada geese by the pond stare as I walk past.

In town, the tail-lifts creak, the pallet trucks squeak and the drunks in the church gardens argue about which of them understands dogs the most. Above them, a fourth-floor window opens and two men lean out. One of them launches a paper dart made from a pizza menu. "What the fuck was that?" the other exclaims as it spiral dives straight down and crashes onto the pavement below.

Later, on the estate, a learner driver cautiously passes the boy of about eight as he jumps from a four-foot-high garden wall using a Morrison's bag as a parachute and then rolls histrionically across the pavement.

I pass two untidy looking men with several missing teeth. They are leaning

on the bins and drinking strong cider. "You look nothing like Postman Pat!" one of them shouts to me in a slightly camp accent. "Do you not like my look?" I ask, "This high-vis is brand new". "It's not so bad, you just don't look like Postman Pat, that's all", the man says before his attention is drawn to the tall woman in her seventies in the full-length woollen overcoat who has just come around the corner and is trying to avoid eye contact. "I love your coat!" he shouts after her. "Thanks, love", says the woman, blushing slightly.

Friday, 13 October

6am: It's been a windy night. There are leaves swirling around the fallen apples on the pavement. In the park, two young men are unable to resist the child's scooter which has been abandoned against a litter bin. After a couple of failed attempts at bunny-hops, they lose interest and prop it back where they'd found it. They are in conversation as they walk up the path towards me: "The thing is, right, she's said a few things recently that have made me feel a bit, hmm". "What? Like it's kind of getting a bit more serious than you'd like?"

I follow the man in head-to-toe hi-vis who is smoking strong weed. He's walking slower than I am and, as I catch him up, he emits a loud belch. When I overtake him and he realises that I'd have been within earshot, he clears his throat several times perhaps thinking I'd assume that what I'd taken to be a noisy eructation was just another attempt at clearing his passages.

The five-year-old plastic lawn at number 12 is really starting to fade now. It has bleached to quite a pale green and is now far more realistic than when it was installed.

The woman in the trouser suit whose long blonde hair is tied back in a black scrunchie is on the phone: "Hiya, can you do us a favour? Can you see if I've

got a bag of Cheetos in the third drawer down?"

On the new estate, three boys are playing football in the road. A girl asks if she can join in, "Yes", says the boy in the Chelsea kit, "You can pretend you're watching us on the TV".

The vicar has installed a lurid 3D picture of a blond haired Christ adjacent to the front door of the vicarage.

It's a bit rough around here; the land-lords have attached advertisements for boarding-up services to the front windows and, at the cash machine outside the post office, an elderly woman wearing Superman pyjamas is withdrawing a tenner.

In town, it's gloomy, wet and windy. I move aside for the three drunks and their free-range bow-legged Staffy. They are owning the space like their lives depend on it—which they probably do. They gob on the floor and ostentatiously impart their observations on life: "She were a right big lass for a girl".

Robbie Williams spills out over 'The Piazza' on the rubbish PA system: "I got too much life running through my veins" he sings with no bottom-end to all the old women as they hobble past Poundworld with their bags-for-life and their hoods up against the pissing horizontal rain.

Saturday, 11 November

As I exit the park gates, I hear a loud crunch. I look up to see a green fluo-rescent cyclist bounce off the side of an Octavia taxi and onto the road. He gets to his feet quickly and holds out his hands in a 'What the fuck?' gesture to driver behind the wheel. "I've got a light", he shouts, switching the light on his helmet off and on again, "I've got a fluorescent jacket", he says, tugging at the collar of his hi-vis, "How come you didn't see me?" The taxi driver doesn't respond.

I follow the two Polish men in anoraks and combat pants down Fitzwilliam Street. The shorter of them is swigging Polish lager as they walk. When they reach the bottom of the hill, he throws his can into the bin and they stand conversing loudly for a minute or so before heading off in opposite directions.

The short tubby man in his late fifties with the raglan cardigan and combover tells me he accidentally went to Whitby during the goth weekender. "By 'eck, we saw some right sights!" he explains, shaking his head. "They were selling steam punk starter kits for twenty quid: a pair of goggles and a hat with a feather in it. I have to admit I was tempted, but I didn't bother in the end."

At the edge of the wood, a five-bar gate has been installed on new wooden posts a couple of metres back from the original stone ones. I open it and make my way up the dirt road past the old stone buildings whose roofs are bright green with moss.

A jay flies out from Southernwood.

The man in the red North Face jacket flicks the bottom of his crisp bag with his middle finger before tipping his head back and upending the dregs into his open mouth.

The tall poplars behind the new estate are capped yellow with the last of the leaves that still cling to the very top of the canopy. There are pink, lace-up Hunter wellingtons, Union Jack themed soft furnishings and a man in a gilet in his late fifties. "There's always something to do", he tells me. "Last weekend I had to unblock the drain and this weekend, I had to build a shed. There's always summat to do, in't there? There's always summit."

Mr Briggs pulls up in his Suzuki Carry: "If you don't see me tomorrow, hang on to my mail, will you? I've got a bloody funeral to go to". And with that, he spins his wheels on the wet leaves in the gutter and speeds away towards Meltham—where it's a right bugger to park, so he often tells me.

The bald man behind me on the bus says he doesn't get why everyone is still bothered about iPhones: "I could understand it when they first came out and you could get an app that made a whipping sound or a noise like a fart; it was fun, but where do you go from there? I mean, what's the point now?"

Wednesday, 20 December

5.30am: It's cold. I don't go through the park because it's too icy and too dark in there. Instead, I duck under the overhanging holly at the entrance and walk around. I edge along glistening pavements, past frozen crisp packets, polystyrene cups and shimmering vomit, sticking close to the railings so I can grab them when I slip.

An old man who smells of weed stops me in the street to wish me a happy Christmas. He puts his hand on my shoulder and hums a short tune. "What's that then?" I ask. "Music" he says, and he wanders off over the road.

At the house with the broken satellite dish and an empty Foster's can in the garden, the front door has been graffitied with a marker pen: inside a wonky love heart it says, "I miss you Mum".

Two young men in grey tracksuits and snapback baseball caps walk past drinking lager and listening to loud auto-tuned pop on mobile speakers with no bottom end.

Outside the Polish Corner restaurant in town, a chubby man in a tracksuit is pretending to buff-up his bald head while he takes a selfie. His friends can barely contain their mirth.

The woman on the bus recommends the Wills O' Nats pub, "The staff really look after you", she says. "Really nice food, really nice atmosphere. It was just nice to get home afterwards."

At the shop, a man is complaining about the self-service checkout: "This isn't working, love. Must be manned by a woman", he says to the female assistant. "You've put your card in upside down", she explains.

Tuesday, 23 January 2018

I'm gagging on the stench of the fetid urine and marinated faeces at the house of the bow-legged terrier called Diesel while over the road a woman in bunny slippers and a bath robe is jumping up and down in a wheelie bin.

A young man in a hoodie sings loudly to himself as he walks past.

Eleven magpies and a crow overlook the estate where pretend owls outnumber the human population by two to one: fluorescent silk flowers in tiny porches, pizza sized ha'penny stepping stones, a row of three tiny retrievers with placards around their necks saying 'Welcome'. Both the Buddha and the donkey that pulls the little wooden cart have lost their heads in the recent frost.

The murky horses look dejected in the steep miry field

Mr Briggs answers his door, legs akimbo, thumbs in belt loops. There are no pleasantries, no hello or good morning, instead, he opens with "Well, he's right in amongst 'em now, in't he?" "Who, What?" I ask. He nods at his neighbour's house over the road, "He's in Goa, in't he? Moans like hell about 'em when they come over here, then he goes over there to see them!"

Ensnared black plastic flaps from barbed wire while a solitary starling swanee whistles from a telegraph pole. A long

'V' formation of geese honk overhead. I pull up in the van next to the field of jackdaws and rooks—hundreds probably. I get out and slam the door. The jackdaws fly off. The rooks stay put.

Sunday, 25 February

It's the first clear blue day for weeks on the solid and dependable streets of semis: half brick, half pebbledash. Reliable men polish hatchbacks or further fine-tune already solid fixtures and fittings. King Charles spaniels bask on the backs of settees. There's no dog shit, no litter. People stop me to talk about the weather. A woodpigeon calls against the gentle background thrum of the busy motorway tributary. Left, into a side street and a step up the aspirational ladder: double bay windows, dormers, steeply pitched roofs, 4x4s on the drives. There are sparrows in the neatly trimmed hedges and there are children in the schoolyard. An elderly woman waits for the Cairn terrier in the little red dog coat to shit under the hedge at the edge of the pavement, her walking stick decorated with souvenir badges. "What a lovely morning!" she says, before bending down to carefully package the mess.

Meanwhile, on the other side of town, the owner of the pornographic bookshop is unloading bulk bought dog food systems from a battered Transit van, his Yorkshire terrier tethered to the door handle. A noisy Subaru Impreza farts past at about 60mph with an acid green quad bike in noisy pursuit. Further down, opposite the house with the brass plaque on the front door that reads, 'A friend in need is a pain in the arse', a couple are huddled over a phone taking an online quiz at the bus stop next to the pile of energy drink cans. "What's the day after Pancake Day?" asks the man. "Valentine's Day", says the woman.

Photographs

p.101: Canal, graffiti, warehouse, gas tower.
p.102: Signs in window, coughs and sneezes... CATCH IT BIN IT KILL IT.
p.105: TV set in road.
p.106: Farmyard sale.
p.109: Bald biker looking in pawn shop window.
p.110: Fog in valley bottom, moors in background.
p.113: Foggy view across valley.
p.114: Modified scooter, wheelie bins, fridge freezer.
p.117: Elevated view of railway station and warehouse.
p.118: Funny cypress trees, suburban semis.
p.121: Victorian terrace, overgrown garden, washing on line.
p.122: Dumped three piece suite, garage, litter.

Some remarks on *Round About Town*

"The funniest book I read this year was the one-man mass-observation of *Round About Town* by Kevin Boniface, a Yorkshire postman with a poet's eye."
—Jeremy Noel-Tod, 'Books of the Year 2018' *Times Literary Supplement*

"There are sandstone streets, specifics of litter, non-sequitur asides from path-crossing neighbours and details, details, sharp and alive. But make no mistake, this is not dour, northern observational humour, this is crisp packet peacocks, the full dynamic range of flora and fauna of an ecosystem both urban and rural elevated to art in the fluttering uncertainty of an eye-blink. This is Rorschach Yorkshire. This is how questions are asked and identity is formed through what you see, through what you hear and what you write. Is this how you find yourself? Or how you lose yourself?"
—Lee Ashworth, *Louder Than War*

"There's no story here, in this whole book, but there are glimpses of hundreds of stories. It is funny, and unsettling, and comforting, often at the same time, and you don't get to find out what happens next."
—Anna Wood, *Caught by the River*

"Instead of being fixed in a frame like a painting, Huddersfield becomes a fluid entity as a series of images, vignettes, incidents and glimpsed lives flow through every page, endlessly unfolding… The book takes everything as it comes. There is no hierarchy of objects or a sense that certain objects and entities are more picturesque or culturally valid than others."
—Gareth E. Rees, *Unofficial Britain*

"*Round About Town* is a work that can conjure fury at poverty, contempt for the poverty of mainstream popular culture and joy at its moments of poetic collapse."
—Phil Smith, *Mythogeography*

"Absurdity lurks around every corner."
—Michael Caines, *Times Literary Supplement*